LONDON UNDERGROUND ROLLING STOCK

BRIAN HARDY

Capital Transport

AUTHOR'S NOTE

Since the last edition of this book some four years ago, refurbishment work has been completed on the Bakerloo, Victoria and with the C69/77 stocks on the Circle, Hammersmith & City and District lines. Similar work is taking place with the Metropolitan Line's A60/62 stock, now three-quarters complete, and the Piccadilly Line's 1973 stock. The Central Line has been fully equipped with 1992 stock and deliveries of new trains for the Northern and Jubilee lines (the 1995 and 1996 stocks respectively) are now in progress. Four-car trains of refurbished A60 stock will return to the East London Line in 1998 when it reopens after resignalling and tunnel refurbishment.

We also include, for the first time, details of the Distribution Services road vehicles. The fleet is owned and managed as part of London Underground. Many of its vehicles are in LUL corporate livery and most are used for LUL business in support and emergency roles. Thanks are due to Kim Rennie for compiling this section, and for the help given by Liz Hendon and Peter Forsdick of Distribution Services.

This book is not an official publication of London Underground Limited and opinions expressed are thus those of the author. Thanks are given to those who have contributed and offered advice especially to London Underground rolling stock engineering and depot staff, the London Transport Museum, photographic contributors and many others. Thanks are also given to Colin Tipp, Manager, Mail Rail, for the latest information on the Post Office Railway, and to Jeanne Hardy for assisting with the typing and checking the typescript.

The London Underground Railway Society publishes regular rolling stock information in its monthly magazine 'Underground News', to enable its members to keep the information in this book up to date. Details of membership can be obtained by post from the Hon. Secretary at 54 Brinkley Road, Worcester Park, Surrey, KT4 8JF.

The information in this book is correct to mid-June 1997.

Ickenham, Middlesex, July 1997 BRIAN HARDY

First published 1976
Fourteenth edition 1997

ISBN 185414 193 7

Published by Capital Transport Publishing, Harrow, HA3 5JL
Printed by CS Graphics, Singapore

© Brian Hardy and Capital Transport Publishing 1997

Overleaf 1992 and 1996 Tube Stock in Ruislip Depot. *John Glover*
D stock at South Kensington. *Capital Transport*

CONTENTS

Passenger rolling stock and engineer's trains working side by side, during weekend track replacement. On 12th November 1995 such work was taking place on the Piccadilly Line near South Ealing, this photograph being taken from Ascott Avenue. On the left is a train of 1973 Tube Stock heading for Heathrow on the westbound 'local' line. The work is taking place on the 'fast' lines, and the engineers' train with battery locomotives is standing on the eastbound line. *Paul Bradley*

INTRODUCTION

London Underground Ltd operates two main types of passenger rolling stock on its railways. One is known as surface stock and is built to full-size gauge for use on the Metropolitan, Circle, Hammersmith & City, District and East London lines, whose tunnel sections are double-tracked and built just below surface level. The other type, tube stock, is used on the Bakerloo, Piccadilly, Northern, Jubilee, Central and Victoria lines, which have deep-level single track tunnels of about 12ft diameter. The new tube tunnels on the Jubilee Line extension east of Green Park are, however, built to a diameter of 14ft.

In the case of tube stock, the different groups are distinguished by the year of anticipated delivery at the time of ordering. Surface stock is distinguished by letters and the last two digits of the year of anticipated delivery. The District Line stock, now officially known as D stock, was originally designated D78 stock and the latter often prevails.

Each train is composed of one or more units coupled together as necessary to form trains of the required length. Units are formed of a number of motor cars and trailer cars semi-permanently coupled. Each unit is self-sufficient as regards current supply for motors, lighting, compressed air supply and auxiliary equipment. Some stocks have units which cannot be operated in service on their own, as they have a driver's cab at one end only, with a shunting control panel at the other. The Central Line's 1992 Tube Stock also has some units which have a shunting control panel at each end and therefore these are always two-car formed in the middle of trains.

The different types of car are:

DM   Driving Motor car, having traction motors and a driver's cab.

NDM   Non-Driving Motor car; as DM but without a driver's cab.

UNDM Uncoupling Non-Driving Motor car; as NDM but provided with control cabinet at one end to allow uncoupling and shunting of a unit without loss of space incurred by a full-size cab.

T   Trailer car; without motors or cab.

To assist in identification, the end cars of units are referred to as 'A' cars (which normally face north or west) or 'D' cars (south or east). Car numbering is also arranged so that distinction can not only be made between 'A' and 'D' cars but also between the types of car and stock. To simplify shunting operations in Stonebridge Park depot, the arrangements on the Bakerloo Line are opposite to that just described. It should be noted, however, that on lines that have loops at terminal stations (Kennington on the Northern Line and Heathrow on the Piccadilly Line) or have triangular junction layouts (for example Rickmansworth-Croxley-Moor Park on the Metropolitan Line), trains will become turned and may face the opposite direction to that mentioned above. The new trains on the Central Line, however, are fully reversible and are not identified with the 'A' and 'D' nomenclature.

Over the period, 1984–1995, all trains, apart from those on the Northern Line, have become one-person operated. The entry into service later in 1997 of the new 1995 Tube Stock on the Northern Line will see the end of guards completely on London's Underground – probably by 1999.

The line allocations of the different types of stock, including spares, are as shown below as in June 1997.

Bakerloo Line	1972 MkI stock	4 trains
	1972 MkII stock	32 trains *
Jubilee Line	1983 stock (batch I)	14 trains
	1983 stock (batch II)	16½ trains
Central Line	1992 stock	85 trains *
Waterloo & City Line	1992 stock	5 trains
Northern Line	1959/62 stock	78½ trains
	1972 MkI stock	20 trains
Piccadilly Line	1973 stock	87 trains *
Victoria Line	1967 stock	39½ trains
	1967/72 stock (converted)	3½ trains *
District Line	C69/77 stock	11 trains §
	D stock	75 trains
H&C and Circle lines	C69/77 stock	35 trains
Metropolitan Line	A60/62 stock	56½ trains †

* Includes withdrawn/damaged stock extant.

† Single four-car units operate on the East London Line, at present closed for rebuilding, to reopen in 1998.

§ Edgware Road-Olympia/Wimbledon section.

The 1959 Tube Stock on the Northern Line is now approaching withdrawal upon entry into service of new 1995 Tube Stock. A train enters Finchley Central in April 1997. *John Glover*

Opposite: The 1962 Tube Stock was built for the Central Line, but a few units now work on the Northern Line. DM 1424 leads a northbound Northern Line train into West Finchley. Note that on 1962 stock, the stabling light is to the left of the headlights. To the top right of the windscreen wiper can be seen an aluminium patch, which has covered up the former 'Central Line' identity. *John Glover*

1959/62 TUBE STOCK

Although first conceived in 1951, financial constraints of the period meant that it was not until 1954 that London Transport was able to consider replacing the Pre-1938 Tube Stock on the Piccadilly Line. In that year, three seven-car prototype trains were ordered, one each from Metro-Cammell, Birmingham and Gloucester, known as 1956 Prototype Tube Stock. These trains were really an updated version of the 1938 stock (which themselves had prototypes in 1935), but new features included rubber suspension of the bogies and wheels, unpainted aluminium exteriors and interior fluorescent lighting in the form of twin tubes along the ceiling centre. Other innovations included improved mercury retarders and e.p. braking, retractable shoegear, rubber window surrounds, flat (instead of grooved) door runners and outside door indicator lights to identify doors not closing properly. The interior colour scheme was officially dove grey but was akin to a light blue. Although the main seating capacity was the same as on 1938 stock, changes were made to the transverse seats in the centre bay, which were re-arranged in facing pairs. At the trailing ends of the cars, there was one tip-up seat on driving motor cars for use by the guard, locked out of use when not required. On DM cars a redesigned roof dome allowed the provision of a roller destination blind above the cab door, which was illuminated by a fluorescent tube from behind. Although the three trains had minor visible differences, all were operationally compatible.

Following successful trials with the 1956 prototypes, which entered service on the Piccadilly Line from September 1957, a total of 76 seven-car trains of 1959 Tube Stock then followed to replace the same number of Pre-1938 stock trains on the Piccadilly Line. The 76 new trains were very similar to their 1956 counterparts but twin headlamps superseded the five marker lights of the 1956 cars, as headcodes on trains were no longer required. The first train entered service on 14th December 1959. Driving motor cars were numbered 1012–1315 ('A' end even numbers and 'D' end odd numbers), trailers 2012–2314 (even numbers only) and non-driving motor cars 9013–9313 (every alternate odd number).

While the 1959 stock was being delivered there was a change of plan regarding the replacement of the Pre-1938 stock on the Central Line. It was proposed to use a new design of rolling stock for that line for which three prototype trains (1960 Tube Stock) had been ordered. Because of the anticipated increase in passenger traffic from the Eastern Region electrification of its suburban routes into Liverpool Street, there would have been insufficient time to test the prototypes thoroughly and it was decided to deliver the last 57 trains of 1959 stock to the Central as a stop-gap measure. As each Central Line train formation is made up of eight cars (two four-car units), an additional 57 non-driving motor cars were ordered from Metro-Cammell in order to lengthen these 57 trains from seven to eight cars. The first eight-car train of 1959 stock entered service on the Central Line on 25th July 1960, although two seven-car trains had been at work on the line from March 1960 for crew training purposes, entering service on 19th April. An order for more trains was placed with the Birmingham Railway Carriage & Wagon Company for 338 driving motor cars and 112 non-driving motor cars, and with the British Railways workshops at Derby for 169 trailers. As Birmingham were unable to fulfil their contract, their order was subsequently transferred to Metro-Cammell. The stock for the Central Line was designated 1962 Tube Stock but deliveries continued without interruption when the 1959 stock was completed, and the first train entered service on 12th April 1962. The two stocks were almost identical in appearance and design and, despite slight variations in equipment, continue to be interchangeable in service.

The delivery of the 1962 stock allowed the 57 trains of 1959 stock to be returned to their rightful line, less the 57 additional non-driving motor cars which were reformed into 1962 stock trains – these had been numbered from new in the 1962 stock series. All 1959 stock had been transferred to the Piccadilly Line by mid-1964. Three additional eight-car and one three-car train of 1962 stock were ordered and delivery followed on from the main batch of 1962 stock. The three eight-car trains were required to replace the same number of 1960 prototype stock trains then on the Central Line that were required for trials with Automatic Train Operation. The additional three-car unit was for the Piccadilly Line's Holborn-Aldwych shuttle service. The numbers of the 1962 stock motor cars were 1400–1751, trailers 2400–2750 (even numbers only) and non-driving motors 9401–9749 (odd numbers only and including the 57 cars of 1959 stock). In all a total of 1,256 cars made up the 1956/59/62 stock family and these can be summarised as follows:

	DM	T	NDM	Total
1956 TUBE STOCK				
Metro-Cammell	4	2	I	7
Gloucester	4	2	I	7
Birmingham	4	2	I	7
Total 1956 Tube Stock	**12**	**6**	**3**	**21**
1959 TUBE STOCK				
Metro-Cammell for Piccadilly Line	304	152	76	532
Metro-Cammell for Central Line	–	–	57	57
Total 1959 Tube Stock	**304**	**152**	**133**	**589**
1962 TUBE STOCK				
Metro-Cammell – Main Batch	338	–	112	450
Derby Works – Main Batch	–	169	–	169
Metro-Cammell – 1960 Stock Replacement	12	–	6	18
Derby Works – 1960 Stock Replacement	–	6	–	6
Metro-Cammell – Aldwych Branch	2	–	–	2
Derby Works – Aldwych Branch	–	I	–	I
Total 1962 Tube Stock	**352**	**176**	**118**	**646**
Grand Total 1956/59/62 Tube Stock	**668**	**334**	**254**	**1256**

In general, the 1959 stock was always associated with the Piccadilly Line and the 1962 stock with the Central Line, but there have been a few occasions when stock from one line has worked on the other and vice versa, albeit for short periods of time.

In 1970–71 trailer cars of both stocks were fitted with de-icing equipment, enabling fluid from a special tank under the car to be spread onto the current rails to prevent ice forming. In addition, small wire brushes can be lowered to sweep the current rails clear of snow. Such cars are identified by having the letter 'D' under or beside the car number. The equipment is controlled by switches in the driver's cab. Another modification made around the same time was the fitting of electric stabling lights on DM cars, to replace oil tail lamps. These were fitted beside the twin headlights, the 1959 stock on the side nearest the centre cab door, the 1962 stock on the opposite side because of the location of the motor alternator indicator.

A seven-car train of 1959 stock was refurbished internally in 1992/93, consideration being given at the time to update the existing fleet rather than to order new trains. This view is of DM car 1028 looking towards the guard's position, whose operating panel can be seen on either side of the communicating door. *Alan Kybird*

Trailer 2266 pauses at Embankment, on the northbound Northern Line, sporting its interior 'garland green' colour scheme unique to that unit. This is one of a number of trials carried out in 1989–90 to enhance interior appearance, other colours trialled being 'country cream', yellow and 'catkin' (a different shade of yellow). In the end 25 other units were painted cream until a decision was made not to do any further interior repainting on overhauls. *Capital Transport*

Construction of the extension of the Piccadilly Line from Hounslow West to serve Heathrow Airport started in 1971 and new rolling stock was ordered for the Piccadilly Line – the 1973 Tube Stock. The commissioning of the 1973 stock started in 1975 and allowed the 1959 stock to be transferred to the Northern Line, then replacing the remaining 1938 stock and allowing the release of 1972 MkII stock to the Bakerloo/ Jubilee. These transfers started in November 1975 and were completed in October 1979.

During the early 1980s, the outer driving cabs of 1959 stock were fitted with train radio for two-way communication between the driver and the line controller, a modification which was later made to the Central Line's 1962 stock. Changes in rolling stock requirements during the 1980s saw some trains of 1959 stock operating on the Bakerloo line between 1983 and 1989.

To celebrate the centenary of electric tube railways, of which the Northern Line section between Borough and Stockwell is part of the original City & South London Railway, one train of 1959 stock was painted in 1990 into 1923 style livery. This comprises Underground train red with maroon doors, grey roof, cream around the saloon windows and around the trailing ends of the cars and black lining. The interior has been painted cerulean blue (which actually looks 'green') and upholstery is 1920's style. The painting work was done by Vic Berry of Leicester and the train re-entered service in its new guise on 19th July 1990. A trial interior refurbishment was carried out on units 1028+1043 and was painted in LUL's new corporate 'red doors' livery, entering service in its new form on 15th June 1993.

New 1992 stock began to enter service on the Central Line from April 1993 and since then, much of the 1962 stock has been scrapped. The last train of 1962 stock operated on the Central Line on 17th February 1995. A small number of trains, however, were transferred to the Northern Line during 1993–94, which enabled the 1956 prototypes to be scrapped, the last in June 1996. A few continue to survive on special duties, for experimental purposes and for track inspections.

The 1959/62 stock trains on the Northern Line will be replaced from late summer 1997 by new 1995 Tube Stock, ending a tradition in rolling stock that had origins dating back to prototypes built in the mid-1930s.

To celebrate the Centenary of the City & South London Railway in 1990, of which the present Northern Line is part, a seven-car train of 1959 Tube Stock was painted in 1920's Underground livery and similarly restored internally. Leading at West Finchley is DM 1031 which used to be numbered 1085. *Mike McCabe*

The trial refurbishment train of 1959 stock, painted in LUL corporate livery, is seen descending from East Finchley and about to enter the tube tunnels. *Brian Hardy*

Below: Three withdrawn units of 1962 Tube Stock were converted into Pilot units, to move new trains of 1995 and 1996 stock. Unit 1570 was painted into olive green livery and NDM 9571 remains in this. It is seen at Ruislip depot. *Capital Transport*

Left: Sandite dispensing duties on the Central Line are undertaken by former 1962 stock NDM 9459, which is formed to make a five-car 1962 stock unit. The car in its unique livery is seen in Ruislip depot.

All of the 1967 Tube Stock on the Victoria Line has been refurbished, and its completion has allowed
a modest increase in the peak train service. A northbound train arrives at Warren Street.
Capital Transport

1967 TUBE STOCK

As a result of the successful trials with converted 1960 Tube Stock for Automatic Train
Operation (ATO) on the 3.8-mile Central Line branch between Hainault and Woodford, it was decided that the Victoria Line should be operated with automatic trains
from its opening. The system would be very similar to that used on the Central Line
but with some improvements.

The stock for the Victoria Line was built by Metro-Cammell and was formed into
four-car units (M-T-T-M), two such units being required for each train. The double-
width car windows and 'pull down' ventilators are features carried on from the 1960
stock motor cars. The passenger door windows are extended upwards to improve the
vision for standing passengers, an idea tried out on 1938 stock car DM 10306 in 1949.
For the train operator, maximum vision has been achieved by the provision of
curved-round cab windows.

Draught screens are set back from the door openings and the interior seating on
DM cars is for 40 passengers. Trailer cars have longitudinal seats in the centre bay
instead of transverse ones, providing a greater standing area, but the seating capacity
is reduced in consequence to 36. Powerful headlights are fitted on the driving motor
cars, one on each side of the front cab door and in addition to the twin red tail lights
a stabling light is fitted. Illuminated advertisement panels were originally provided
in all cars.

The bright interior of 1967 stock following refurbishment, showing the use of the line colour for handrails. *Capital Transport*

A combined 'traction/brake controller' is provided in the cab which takes the place of separate equipment for motoring and braking, with all such positions required being provided on one handle. A hydraulic handbrake, one of which is capable of holding a loaded train on the steepest gradient, was provided in each cab, but these have now been replaced by spring applied parking brakes. Because of the additional equipment provided on this stock (for ATO and for rheostatic braking), the motor alternator is located on the trailer cars. A 'vigilance' button was provided for manual driving.

Other innovations include a public address system, a 'carrier wave' communication system whereby the train operator can speak directly to the signal operator in Cobourg Street (Euston) control room (since superseded by train radio), a yellow 'calling on' light that can be illuminated to call a following train on for assistance, and communication between cabs on the train enabling the operator to speak to station staff at the rear of the train if the need arises.

The contract for the 1967 stock was placed in March 1964 and the original order was for 122 driving motor cars (61 'A' end north cars 3001–3061 and 61 'D' end south cars 3101–3161) and 122 trailers (4001–4061 and 4101–4161) to operate between Walthamstow and Victoria. The first four-car unit was delivered to Ruislip depot on 27th September 1967. When the extension south from Victoria to Brixton was authorised, an additional 36 motor cars (3062–3079 and 3162–3179) and 36 trailers (4062–4079 and 4162–4179) were ordered from Metro-Cammell, identical to the first batch.

After being delivered to Ruislip depot and following commissioning, most units of 1967 stock were transferred to Hainault depot for ATO trials between Hainault and Woodford in single four-car formations. The first to enter passenger service was unit 3009 on 21st February 1968. After these trials they were transferred to the Victoria Line depot at Northumberland Park for storage until the new line became operational, the first train to arrive comprising units 3009 and 3011 on 1st April 1968. Enough trains had reached Northumberland Park to operate the first stage of the line, which was opened between Highbury & Islington and Walthamstow Central on 1st September 1968.

The dramatic increase in passenger traffic in the mid-1980s required London Underground to consider additional trains for the Victoria Line service. Plans were drawn up to create an additional seven four-car units by converting some units of 1972 MkI stock from the Northern Line. This was done at Acton Works between 1987 and 1989. The additional units are single-ended, the 1972 cars being formed in the middle of eight-car trains. The work not only involved the renumbering of the 1972 converted cars, but also some of the 1967 stock cars involved with the scheme, which gave 32 'A' end, 32 'D' end and 22 double-ended four-car units, making a line total of 43 eight-car trains, 3½ more than hitherto. Two motor-trailer pairs were also converted from 'D' cars to 'A' cars and those involved can be found in the renumbering section later in this book.

During 1989 and into early-1990 all 43 Victoria Line trains were modified at Acton Works by having 'passenger alarm' push buttons fitted, along with improved safety features. A new spring-applied parking brake replaced the original hydraulic hand-brake. Two units completed (3061 and 3110) were selected for refurbishment trials, this being done in 1989 by Vic Berry of Leicester and Tickford Rail. The interiors were completely gutted and new lighting, seating, flooring, stylish panelling and grab rails were fitted. The exteriors were painted in a livery of blue above the waist, white below, red front cabs and grey roofs. The train re-entered service on 9th October 1989. It was subsequently decided that the whole Victoria Line fleet of 43 trains should be refurbished, the first train (comprising units 3005 and 3185) being despatched in June 1990. The work was undertaken by Tickford Rail Ltd at Rosyth Royal Dockyard. The exteriors were painted in the new corporate 'red doors' livery – off white with a blue skirt, red cab ends (only on operative cabs, not 'middle' cabs) and grey roofs. Inside, the finished product is similar to the prototype, with refinements, and includes space for fans to be fitted at a later date. Passenger alarm push-buttons have been replaced by handles and an audible door-close bleep has been provided. The Victoria Line light blue colour has been used on grab rails. In the driving cab, improvements have also been made and the old lever-operated door controls have been replaced by push buttons.

The modification work was completed in May 1995, the last train, however, having some different features, the trailing ends of all cars being painted dark grey to improve inner end appearance. Unit 3186 has been modified to provide additional standing space; the former double transverse seats have been reduced to 'generous sized' single seats, while in the trailer cars, the four seats in the centre section next to the doorways have been replaced by 'perch seats'. In the case of the latter, interior windows are reduced by half but the exterior windows remain the same, although blacked out where they cannot be seen through. Unit 3016 in fact comprises two cars of 1972 Mk I stock (ex 3204 and 4204) which have been converted from 'A' to 'D' cars and renumbered 3116 and 4116 respectively. The original 3116 and 4116 have been converted from 'D' to 'A' cars and renumbered 3016 and 4016, replacing collision damaged cars of the same numbers. The original 4016 has been scrapped, while the disposal of the original 3016 is imminent.

Only 20 trains of the 1972 MkI Tube Stock remain as crew-operated trains on the Northern Line, and even their days are numbered now that the 1995 Tube Stock is being delivered. The remainder have either been converted to work on the Victoria and Bakerloo lines. although a small number have been scrapped. A seven-car train is seen approaching Woodside Park, with DM 3521 leading. The car has acquired a blue-painted door from one of the painted trains. *John Glover*

1972 TUBE STOCK

The Northern Line's 1972 MkI stock is very similar in appearance to the 1967 stock on the Victoria Line, but was built for crew operation. The stock is formed into three- and four-car units, one of each being required for each train (M-T-T-M+UNDM-T-M). The shunting control equipment for the uncoupling non-driving motor cars was obtained from withdrawn 1938 and 1949 tube stock UNDMs.

The total order comprised 90 driving motor cars, 90 trailers and 30 uncoupling non-driving motor cars, all in unpainted aluminium. The stock is numbered 3201–3230 ('A' end DMs), 3301–3330 ('D' end DMs), 3501–3530 ('D' end DMs with mechanical couplers only), 4201–4230, 4301–4330 and 4501–4530 (trailers) and 3401–3430 (UNDMs). External door-indicator lights were fitted, now a standard item on new stock. The first train entered service on the Northern Line on 26th June 1972 (units 3202 and 3502).

A further order for 1972 stock was later placed with Metro-Cammell for an additional 33 trains (known as 1972 MkII stock) and comprised 99 driving motor cars, 99 trailers and 33 uncoupling non-driving motor cars. The MkII stock is numbered 3231–3263 ('A' end DMs), 3331–3363 ('D' end DMs), 3531–3563 ('D' end DMs with mechanical couplers only), 4231–4263, 4331–4363 and 4531–4563 (trailers) and 3431–3463 (UNDMs). This second batch provided the rolling stock for stage one of the Jubilee Line which was opened to the public from 1st May 1979. Prior to that, it was used on the Northern Line, allowing further 1938 stock trains to be withdrawn. Trains of 1972 MkII stock entered service from 19th November 1973.

Although similar in appearance to the MkI cars, red-painted passenger doors were introduced on the MkII stock and all-red roundels replaced 'Underground' transfers on the motor car sides as well as being introduced on other cars. It was the intention with the 1972 MkII stock for it to be converted to ATO at a later date and at first some trains were provided with a motorised destination blind and electronic train set number equipment. This was soon replaced by the standard train set number plates (in the offside cab window rather than beneath the front cab door window) and hand-operated destination blinds.

When new, the seating moquette of the 1972 MkI stock was red/black/green with red plastic arm rests, while on the MkII, it was green/blue with blue arm rests.

From 1977 trains of 1972 MkII stock, displaced by the 1959 stock on the Northern Line, began working on the Bakerloo Line in readiness for the Stanmore branch becoming the Jubilee Line in 1979. The transfer process was a gradual one, completed in time for the opening of the Jubilee Line between Stanmore and Charing Cross on 1st May 1979. In the interim period, the 1972 MkII stock worked all over the Bakerloo Line, including to and from Watford Junction.

Following the service reductions of December 1982, four MkII trains were returned to the Northern Line during 1983 and were modified so that they were compatible with the MkI type. The first train with a combination of the two types ran on the Northern Line on 12th September 1983 (units 3210 and 3533).

With the entry into service of the 1983 stock on the Jubilee Line, a further 14 trains of 1972 MkII stock made their way to the Northern Line between November 1984 and November 1985. This allowed the 1938 stock to be withdrawn from the Bakerloo Line, by transferring more trains of 1959 stock from the Northern Line.

In June 1985 unit 3203–4203–4303–3303 was withdrawn from service, providing the spares necessary for overhauling the 1972 stock fleet at Golders Green Depot, which started in September 1985. This included the Jubilee Line's allocation of 1972 MkII stock, which necessitated transfer between Neasden and Golders Green, completed in early 1987. Following this, Stonebridge Park depot commenced overhauls of the Northern Line's 1972 MkI stock.

The delivery of the 1983 (batch II) stock for the Jubilee allowed the 1972 Mk II stock on that line be transferred to the Bakerloo, which was achieved in March 1989. On the Bakerloo Line, the 1972 Mk II stock operates 'wrong way round', in that the 'D' ends face north and the 'A' ends face south. This allows shunting operations in Stonebridge Park depot to be carried out from a middle (33xx) motor car rather than from an UNDM car. OPO on the Bakerloo Line commenced on 20th November 1989.

To create 3½ additional trains to increase services on the Victoria Line, five four-car and four three-car units of 1972 MkI stock were converted at Acton Works during 1987–89. The four UNDM cars made redundant by this plan have been scrapped although two of them were used in the interim for experiments in refurbishment styles.

During 1989 and into 1990 all 1972 MkI trains on the Northern Line were modified at Acton Works by having 'passenger alarm' buttons fitted, along with improved safety features. A new spring-applied parking brake replaced the original hydraulic handbrake.

Opposite: The Bakerloo Line's 1972 Tube Stock differs cosmetically from the Victoria Line's refurbished trains in having white car numbers above the DM cab windows, as illustrated on a southbound Bakerloo Line train arriving at Willesden Junction. This appears to be on a special working, maybe on one of the occasions that the Bakerloo Line splits into two parts, where the Harrow & Wealdstone service terminates at Queen's Park (and runs empty to Kilburn High Road to reverse). *John Glover*

In 1989, three trains of 1972 MkI stock on the Northern Line were painted in different liveries. The first was blue above waist level (seen at High Barnet), followed closely by the blue doors livery (seen at East Finchley). The livery eventually chosen to be the Corporate standard was the red doors style (seen leaving Edgware). As can be seen, no attempt is now made to keep the painted units together, although the four-car unit of the first train has now been disbanded.
All photos: Alan Kybird

Three trains of 1972 MkI stock on the Northern Line were painted in various trial liveries during 1989. The first to be done comprised units 3204 and 3522, finished in the same style as the Victoria Line prototype described in the previous chapter. This was followed by units 3227 and 3518 which had an all-white body but with blue passenger doors. The final train (units 3202 and 3523) was painted in what has now become London Underground's new corporate standard – the 'red doors' livery.

The refurbishment programme referred to in the previous chapter also included the 1972 stock fleet. Although finished in the same style, line colours (Bakerloo brown and Northern Line black) have been used on some of the interior finishes. Prior to being sent for refurbishment, one Northern Line train of 1972 MkI stock (units 3203 and 3501) was converted to OPO to enable the Bakerloo Line stock to be increased from 33 to 34 trains. Unit 3203 had been out of service since 1985, and was utilised for overhaul spares, while 3501 was being repaired following a collision. To follow in Bakerloo Line numbering sequence, the two units became (respectively) 3264 and 3564.

The refurbishment of the Bakerloo Line's 1972 MkII stock was completed in April 1995 but the Northern Line's MkI refurbishment was stopped after three trains because of the anticipated order of new trains – the 1995 Tube Stock now being delivered. These 1972 MkI trains now form part of the Bakerloo fleet. The work includes OPO conversion and the replacing of interior materials in Bakerloo Line brown. However, they remain distinguishable in retaining the black 'kicking strips' at the bottom of the doors. Units 3218+3507 are now 3265+3565 respectively, 3524 is 3566 and 3210+3512 has become 3267+3567. Unit 3266 in fact comprises cars salvaged from two separate collisions – 3266 and 4266 were 3324 and 4324 (converted from MkI 'D' to 'A' cars) while 4366 and 3366 were MkII cars 4349 and 3349 appropriately renumbered. MkII unit 3539 has also been written off (UNDM 3439 survives as a spare car) and DM 3257 has been scrapped, the other three cars of the unit now being spare although trailer 4257 is in damaged condition.

To summarise, out of the 210 cars of 1972 Mk I stock originally delivered, 140 remain on the Northern Line, 30 are on the Victoria Line, 26 on the Bakerloo Line and 14 have been scrapped. Out of the 231 cars of the 1972 MkII stock, five have been scrapped. At present, it is envisaged that the 1972 MkI stock on the Northern Line will be scrapped when replaced by 1995 Tube Stock.

Left: Interior of a 1972 MkI DM car looking towards the guard's panel. In original condition, the interiors of MkI and MkII stock differed little when built, apart from the seating moquette. The 1972 MkI was red/black/grey while the 1972 MkII was blue/green. Now, the 'Northern Line' moquette is fitted to that line's MkI stock. *Jeanne Hardy*

Right: Interior of refurbished 1972 MkII stock on the Bakerloo Line, featuring some of the decor in the 'line' colour. Note the longitudinal seating in the centre bay, a layout introduced on 1967 and 1972 stock trailers. *Jeanne Hardy*

A refurbished train of 1973 Tube Stock, painted in LUL Corporate colours, enters service from Northfields depot, while an unrefurbished train stands in the siding awaiting its next working.
Brian Hardy

1973 TUBE STOCK

In order to provide new stock for the Piccadilly Line specifically for the Heathrow Airport extension, orders were placed with Metro-Cammell for $87\frac{1}{2}$ six-car trains, comprising 196 driving motor cars, 175 trailers and 154 uncoupling non-driving motor cars. Each car is about six feet longer than cars of earlier stock but the total length of a six-car train is about 17 feet shorter than a seven-car 1956/59 stock train. This enables the complete train to fit into the platforms at all tube stations on the line, necessary as the stock was subsequently converted to one-person operation. The first train entered service on 19th July 1975 as a passenger-carrying special when the extension from Hounslow West to Hatton Cross was opened, formed of units 108 and 137. The first normal passenger working occurred on 18th August 1975, comprising units 140 and 141.

The majority of trains are formed M-T-UNDM+UNDM-T-M. The driving motor cars at each end are provided with mechanical couplers only, the UNDM cars being fitted with automatic couplers. In addition there are 21 three-car units formed M-T-M known as 'double-cab' units, with automatic couplers on each driving motor car.

The purpose of these units is to give fleet flexibility, being able to replace an 'A' or 'D' end single end unit requiring maintenance. One unit was also provided to operate the Holborn-Aldwych shuttle service until closure on 30th September 1994.

The 1973 stock is numbered 100–253 (DMs), 854–895 (DMs with automatic couplers for double-cab units), 300–453 (UNDMs), 500–653 (trailers) and even numbers only from 654–694 (trailers used in double-cab units).

DM 114 of the hybrid unit 114–688–889 has been converted to a double-ended DM proper and the whole unit renumbered 896–696–897 respectively. However, the original 114 can be recognised here, retaining its black roof and seen at Hillingdon. From the end of September 1996, off-peak Piccadilly Line services returned to Uxbridge on a daily basis after an absence of many years.
Brian Hardy

Improvements introduced on this stock were the provision of air-operated cab doors, being operated independently from the passenger doors; a selective-open facility enabling in bad weather all except one single door and one single leaf of a double door on each car to remain closed at terminal stations; the Westcode electro-pneumatic braking system, enabling the Westinghouse air brake to be omitted; a train equipment fault-finding panel for the driver's use; automatic wheel slip/slide protection and load control of acceleration and braking. The motor alternator (located on the trailer cars of 1967 and 1972 stocks) is fitted on the driving motors (as on 1962 stock and before) and UNDMs.

On all 1973 stock cars, the interior seating is arranged longitudinally at each end, with transverse seats in the centre bay, each type of car seating 44 passengers. Sliding ventilators are provided above the car windows. The train set number panel has numbers of the 'flapper' type. The driving end of each DM car has a red painted section below the cab windows, extending around the side to meet the edge of the cab door. The intention to fit three ceiling-mounted fans on each car was hampered by design difficulties and it was not until October 1977 that fans were first used. Even so they were not wholly successful – not all cars were fitted and those that were have now been decommissioned. A total of 25 single-ended 'A' units were fitted from new with de-icing equipment. Small detail differences existed on the trains when they were new, the first 16 units (100–115) having black roofs and a total of 22 units (100–117, 178, 179, 202 and 203) having higher waist-level joint lines than the rest of the fleet.

The reason for the construction of the 1973 stock was the extension to serve Heathrow Airport. This was completed for opening on 16th December 1977, when Her Majesty the Queen opened the section from Hatton Cross to Heathrow Central (now known as Heathrow Terminals 1,2,3). The special train, carrying a special headboard, comprised units 244+245 which entered passenger service later that day.

The last two double-cab units of 1973 stock were built for experimental purposes, cars 892–692–893 having Westinghouse equipment and 894–694–895 having GEC equipment. The two units were known as the Experimental Tube Train (ETT) and testing with unit 892 on the South Ealing test tracks commenced in 1978.

Having high-tech non-standard equipment, it was necessary for the train to be 'piloted' to and from the test tracks for which a three-car unit of 1938 stock (10306–

In an experiment to generate extra revenue, one six-car train of 1973 Tube Stock was painted into all-over advertisement livery for United Airlines, re-entering service on 19th June 1995. It is seen at Rayners Lane on an eastbound Piccadilly Line working. Special seating moquette was fitted in August 1995, but otherwise the interior is unchanged. *Brian Hardy*

012498–11247) was specially adapted, being based at Northfields depot. Unit 892 was transferred to Hainault in February 1979 for testing on the Hainault-Woodford branch and it entered occasional passenger service from 25th July 1983. Testing of unit 894 commenced in September 1980, based at Northfields. When the tests were concluded, it was decided to convert the two units to standard, as additional stock would be necessary for the extension of the Piccadilly Line to serve Heathrow Terminal 4. Unit 894 entered Acton Works for conversion in early-1984 and was transferred back to Northfields on 16th August 1985, entering service on 12th February 1986. Unit 892 followed suit, arriving at Acton Works in June 1985. It was returned to Northfields on 10th October 1986, entering service six months later on 10th April 1987.

On 1st April 1986 Their Royal Highnesses the Prince and Princess of Wales officially opened the new Terminal 4 station and buildings at Heathrow Airport, for which 1973 stock units 864 and 195 were used, being given a special headboard and side 'Concorde' stickers, as well as a special 'Terminal 4' destination blind. Passenger services

Interior of unrefurbished 1973 stock. The yellow notices on the draught screens direct tourists to place baggage alongside the doors, an arrangement which has never been very satisfactory and which is being improved by a greater space allocation for luggage on the refurbished trains.
Capital Transport

commenced on 12th April, but Piccadilly Line trains worked non-stop through the new station and around the new single-track loop from the new timetable on 7th April. One-way loop workings cause trains to become 'turned' and unless an even number of trips is worked, which is impossible to guarantee with the operating complexities of the Piccadilly Line, some trains finish at the end of the day the opposite way round. As the 1973 stock is unable to couple 'A' to 'A' and 'D' to 'D' for operational purposes, the two ex-ETT units give additional stock to assist in overcoming the problem of trains stabled the wrong way round.

When unit 114–514–314 was new, it was used (along with 315–515–115) for crew training at Cockfosters. When this was completed the unit was used to provide spares for others already in service. Trailer 514 was used for experiments with ventilation in 1982, while DM 114 replaced DM 888 badly damaged by fire near Bounds Green on 11th August 1992. DM 114 entered service for the first time (with 688 and 889) on 31st March 1983. This left cars 314 and 514 spare, never having entered service. Trailer 514 was acquired to become the purpose-built Track Recording Car for the Underground, being converted by BREL at Derby and completed in the spring of 1987. It was renumbered TRC666 and was painted in the red and white livery carried by its 1960 stock converted pilot motors. UNDM 314 served as a temporary canteen at Northfields in 1984/85, and since then has been used for refurbishment experiments. It was transferred to RFS at Doncaster on 23rd June 1993 for further experiments and onwards to Bombardier at Horbury on 3rd November 1994. Fire damaged DM 888 was scrapped in January 1993; meanwhile, DM 114 was converted to a double ended DM and the whole unit renumbered 896–696–897.

With the transfer of overhauling stock from Acton Works to depots, Cockfosters took on the role for the 1973 stock, the first unit of which (315–515–115) was completed in June 1986. The first of the deep-level tube lines to be converted to one-person operation was the Piccadilly Line, operative from 31st August 1987. The 1973 stock was converted for OPO at Northfields depot (all single-ended units and two double-cab units) and Acton Works (the remaining double-cab units) during 1986 and up to September 1987. The exterior differences include the fitting of an offside window wiper and calling-on light. (When the stock was new, a calling-on light was fitted on the driver's side of the destination blind, but was later replaced by an opening for cab ventilation). In the operator's cab, door control buttons have been provided on the console and a new operator's seat fitted. From 31st August 1987, the date of OPO introduction on the Piccadilly Line, the operation of the passenger emergency alarms system was changed so that drivers could take the train on to the next station in the event of a passenger using the alarm.

Following refurbishment trials on UNDM car 314, three-car unit 190 was chosen for exterior painting and a complete interior refurbishment. This was done by Metro-Cammell at Birmingham and was one of the first units of 1973 stock to have a series of engineering modifications done at Acton Works to improve service reliability. The exterior was painted in the 'red doors' corporate livery, but in a shade of red darker than hitherto. Windows were put in the trailing ends of the cars for added passenger security while each car was given a different layout in the centre bay, which included seats and luggage accommodation. The fitting of door close bleeps meant that unrefurbished unit 123 had to be modified to work with it, the train entering service on 20th January 1991. For a time, DM 190 also had a black-on-yellow dot matrix destination display.

During 1992 and 1993, Correct Side Door Enable equipment was fitted to 1973 stock trains and was introduced on the Picadilly Line from 6th September 1993. Following this modification, the original Train Equipment fault finding panels (TEPs) were replaced with less complex Cab Display Units (CDUs), a programme completed in September 1994.

The contract for refurbishing the 1973 stock was awarded to RFS of Doncaster and

Interior of refurbished 1973 Tube Stock. Although Piccadilly Line blue is widely used, the armrests are in red. Perch seats and luggage space have been installed around the door areas in the centre section of the saloon. End windows have been cut in for passenger security, as seen here, and interior destination indicators are also included. *Capital Transport*

the first two units (866 and 151) were taken from Ruislip depot by road in May 1993. With RFS being absorbed by Bombardier, the train was taken to Bombardier's Horbury site during November and December 1994. Many new features have been incorporated in the refurbishment scheme, which is expected to be complete by the year 2000. The exteriors are painted in Corporate livery, but the cab is grey beneath the cab windows to the top of the headlights. The train set number is now incorporated above the destination area on the cab fronts, while the front cab area comprises a (folded) detraining ladder and lights. The first train re-entered service on 17th June 1996.

Seating is all longitudinal, reducing capacity from 44 to 38. However, perch seats are provided at the car ends and by the door area in the centre bay, greatly enhancing luggage and standing space. Interior dot matrix indicators are provided and pre-set digital voice announcements are available, set by the train operators. In June 1997, a total of 17 refurbished trains were in service. Unit 204–604–404 was damaged in a collision in December 1990 and at one stage it was intended to reinstate it to service but the possibility of additional heavily modified trains of 1983 stock for the Piccadilly Line makes this now unlikely.

The 1973 stock has also been used in trials with inter-car barriers to prevent passenger falls between cars and experiments are taking place with in-cab CCTV for platform monitoring.

1983 TUBE STOCK

The 1983 Tube Stock was originally conceived for what would have been the full-length variously known Fleet, River, or Jubilee Line back in the 1970s, then expected to total 60 or more trains. The decision not to build beyond Charing Cross reduced the total trains required to 33 which would have provided a one-for-one replacement of the 1972 MkII stock, which would be transferred to the Bakerloo Line. As events turned out, and with then declining Underground ridership, only 15 new trains were ordered from Metro-Cammell in 1981, with the balance (by then whittled down to 13 trains) being cancelled in 1982. Each new train was formed of two three-car M-T-M units and numbering is as follows: 'A' DMs 3601–3630, 'D' DMs 3701–3730 and trailers 4601–4630.

The 1983 stock has a number of features that were new to tube stock, some of which had already been incorporated successfully in the District Line D stock. The front of the train has flat but deeper driving cab windows, incorporating shatterproof glass to give greater protection to the driver. Single-leaf doors supersede double doors on all cars and the opening of these is by push-buttons operated by passengers.

The single-leaf doors, along with reduced standback areas by them, enabled seating capacity to be increased from 44 (as on 1973 stock) to 48 per car. The seats are covered in the same moquette as that used previously on District Line D stock (yellow/orange/brown/black). Mustard coloured melamine panelling is fitted inside except at the doorway positions, where orange is used. Because none of the single-leaf doors slide towards the centre of the saloon, the car windows in this section are single glazed. The cars are illuminated by fluorescent tubes, but in the form of 'luminators', which also provide light behind advertisements. Other features include bogies of welded box-frame construction without headstocks and with 'blob' suspension. Traction equipment is by Kiepe and a Programme Logic System (PLS) replaces the Train Equipment Panel in the driver's cab. The cab interior is painted bright blue and a 'fore/aft' traction/brake controller is provided, along with a free-standing adjustable seat for the driver.

Facing page: DM3609 leading at Queensbury is one of only five units of 1983 Tube Stock to retain original closely-spaced vents over the front cab door. *Alan Kybird*

Above: Interior of a 1983 batch I car showing the centre section with a mix of longitudinal and transverse seating. *Capital Transport*

The first three-car unit was delivered to Neasden depot on 27th August 1983, the last arriving on 11th May 1985. The last five units have trailers with de-icing equipment (4626–4630). Normal passenger operation commenced on 8th May 1984 using units 3607 and 3609, but this train made its debut to user groups on 1st May and to the press on 2nd May, the latter occasion also carrying passengers.

In late 1986 authority was given for further trains of 1983 stock, in order to restore rolling stock and services near to pre-December 1982 levels. This new order comprised $16\frac{1}{2}$ six-car trains and was numbered as follows: 'A' DMs 3631–3663, 'D' DMs 3731–3763 and trailers 4631–4663, of which 4631–4635 have de-icing equipment. Although almost identical to the first batch of stock, the 1983 (batch II) differed in that the red/blue Underground bullseye replaced the solid red roundel, car numbers are in blue and interior car lighting is with standard fluorescent tubes, as on 1967/72/73 stocks and not with luminators as on batch I. The first unit of the new order (3636–4636–3736) was received at Neasden depot on 11th October 1987 and entered service (with batch I stock) on 27th November 1987. With the Jubilee Line's imminent conversion to OPO (on 28th March 1988), only five batch II units (3636/7/8/40/1) entered service before then in crew-operated mode. The batch I stock was modified for OPO at Acton Works between October 1986 and August 1987, operating as a crew-operated train in modified form until the changeover date.

The decision to extend the Jubilee Line from Green Park to Stratford via Canary Wharf was taken in 1993, for which a complete fleet of new trains was required – the 1996 Tube Stock now being delivered. The future of the relatively new 1983 stock is thus in doubt, although current plans envisage many of the units stored pending further adaptation for the enhanced services on the Piccadilly Line in the new millennium, should finance become available. However, units 3623–4623–3723 and 3628–4628–3730 have already been withdrawn, the former being scrapped in September 1995.

The Central Line became fully worked by 1992 Tube Stock in February 1995. Since it was new, many modifications have been made, some visible externally. One of the first to be noticed was the fitting of the ATP/tripcock reset bars, which can be seen cutting through the car number, in this case DM 91095 leading at West Acton. *Brian Hardy*

1992 TUBE STOCK

The replacement rolling stock for the Central Line was the result of extensive trials conducted with three four-car prototype trains known as the 1986 Prototype Tube Stock. These three prototypes tested new materials and construction methods and experimented with different interior seating layouts.

Two of the four prototypes were built by Metro-Cammell of Birmingham (trains 'A' and 'C'), the third (train 'B') by BREL Ltd of Derby. Electrical equipment for one of the Metro-Cammell trains was provided by GEC Traction of Manchester and for the other by Brown-Boveri of Zurich, Switzerland. Brush Electrical Machines of Loughborough provided the equipment for the BREL train. Each of the three trains was finished in a distinctive colour and, to give a feeling of spaciousness and security inside, the two Metro-Cammell trains had windows in the car ends. All trains had the side windows extended up into the curve of the roof.

Each of the prototypes consisted of two two-car motored units, one car having a driving cab and the other no cab. The automatic coupling arrangements between units and the controls of all three trains were designed to be compatible so that any combination of two car units could couple to form a four-, six- or eight-car train. The car bodies and the floor structure were constructed from wide aluminium extrusions welded together, which make them both lighter and cheaper to manufacture than tube car bodies built previously. This form of construction requires external sliding doors which do not need 'pockets' in the body structure. Train 'A' was painted red, train 'B' blue and train 'C' green.

The three trains were formed and numbered thus:

Formation:	DM	NDM	+NDM	DM
Train 'A'	11	21	22	12
Train 'B'	13	23	24	14
Train 'C'	15	25	26	16

The three prototypes were delivered in 1986 and 1987 and following extensive testing, the trains operated spasmodically in passenger service between 4th May 1988 and 14th August 1989 in six-car formations on the Jubilee Line. Following some seven years out of use, the prototypes were scrapped between August and October 1996, with the exception of DM 16 of green train 'C', which has been acquired for preservation by the LT Museum.

An order for 85 trains of Central Line Replacement Stock (as it was then known – now the 1992 Tube Stock) was placed in 1989 with BREL of Derby, which became ASEA Brown Boveri (or ABB Transportation Ltd), but is now ADtranz Ltd. Each train of 1992 Tube Stock comprises eight cars formed of four two-car units. There are three combinations of two-car unit and four types of individual vehicle. Car 'A' is a driving motor with cab, shoes, traction equipment and automatic coupler. Car 'B' is a non-driving motor car having no cab or shoes, but has traction equipment which is fed from the adjacent motor car. It also has a shunting control cabinet at its outer end along with an automatic coupler. Car type 'C' is similarly a non-driving motor car having no cab, but has shoes and traction equipment as an 'A' car, along with a shunting control cabinet and automatic coupler at its outer end. De-icing cars are a variation on car type 'C' and are designated as type 'D'. With these four types of car, semi-permanent two-car units are formed as follows: 175 A-B units, 133 B-C units and 32 B-D de-icing units. All the two car units are fully reversible and compatible and thus there is no distinction between 'A' and 'D' ends as hitherto. Car numbering is as follows:

Car type A 91001–91349 odd numbers	Total 175 cars
Car type B 92001–92349 odd numbers in A-B units	
Car type B 92002–92266 even numbers in B-C units	Total 340
Car type B 92402–92464 even numbers in B-C de-icing units	
Car type C 93002–93266 even numbers in B-C units	Total 165 cars
Car type D 93402–93464 even numbers in B-D de-icing units	

With different combination of cars and units, it is possible for an eight-car train to be formed in one of 36 different ways, although current policy keeps DM cars at the outer ends of trains whenever possible.

Each car has all longitudinal seating arranged six per side in the outer bays and five per side in the centre saloon bay (i. e. between the double doors), giving a total of 34 seats per car. The middle pair of each group of six are set back six inches to allow greater standing capacity, at which point there is a floor-to-ceiling grab pole in the centre. At non-cabbed ends (at the trailing end of car 'A' and both ends of cars 'B', 'C'

The ends of B-C two-car units of 1992 Tube Stock are not normally seen by the public, always being in the middle of train formations. NDM 92042 is in Ruislip depot. Note the single head and tail light under the 'shunting' window. *Les Collings*

and 'D') there is one perch seat in each corner position. The interior colour scheme is in soft stone with seating moquette in warm red/ivory/blue arranged in diagonally split squares. Car floors are of rubber type material in grey/blue terrazzo chip. Grab rails are the all-round type as on 1986 prototype train 'A'. The large single-glazed car windows, which curve up into the roof line, have been adopted from the prototype trains.

Passenger door control buttons are provided. 'Open' buttons are in the middle of the door separations inside and out, while extra 'open' buttons are fitted inside to the 'stand-back' pillars, one each side, along with door close buttons. The passenger door width is 1664mm (double) and 832mm (single), each leaf being some 6 inches wider than on the prototype trains to allow speedier alighting and boarding and thereby reducing station stop times. Like the prototype trains, sliding doors are externally hung. Apart from the driving end of the 'A' cars, end windows are provided to give greater security. Other interior features include pre-programmed announcements in digitised speech. The exteriors are painted in corporate livery but the cab front, although red, has the window surrounds dark grey.

The driver's cab incorporates in-cab closed circuit television, provided by Siemens/ BREL. In addition to public address, in the event of an emergency, there is two-way communication between the driver and passengers. The driver has a redesigned fore/aft traction brake controller, which is positioned on the right hand of the driver's seat – reminiscent of that provided on the 1935 streamlined tube stock!

The interiors of all 1992 Tube Stock on the Central and Waterloo & City lines are almost identical. Now devoid of armrests, like most of the stock, this is the interior of DM 65502. *Alan Kybird*

The thyristor controlled traction equipment is provided by a consortium of ASEA Brown Boveri of Switzerland and Brush Electrical Machines of Loughborough. A computer data transmission system with multiplexing is used for much of the electrical control of the trains. This reduces the number of cables but safety circuits such as braking are separately wired as well. The Westinghouse analogue braking system is fitted, along with air suspension. The bogies are provided by Kawasaki Heavy Industries of Osaka, Japan. Each car has six ventilation units giving full forced ventilation.

The length of each car is 16248mm over body ends, 2620mm wide over door leaves and 2869mm high at the top of the car roof. Construction of the new Central Line trains started in the late-summer of 1990 and the first four-car train to be delivered arrived at Ruislip depot on 17th May 1992. A three-car unit of 1962 stock (1422–9423–1423) was fitted with redundant compressors from the 1986 stock and was used as a pilot unit for transferring test units of 1992 stock between Ruislip and Northfields.

The first train entered passenger service on the Central Line on 7th April 1993. With only two trains outstanding to be delivered, enough were available for the full Monday to Friday service to be worked with new trains from Monday 20th February 1995.

Since new, a number of visible and audible changes and modifications have been made to the 1992 stock fleet. First was the fitting of tripcock/ATP reset bars beneath the driver's window enabling resetting to be done without the Train Operator having to get down onto the track – the first stage of Automatic Train Protection commenced on the western branches to North Acton on 19th June 1995. The unreliability of the illuminated train set number and destination display equipment led to their replacement by early-1996 and by mid-1996 respectively. In the case of the latter, it was necessary to carry card destination indicators in the front cab door for a year or so. The audible 'door open' bleeps gave way to a single bleep by early-1996, this modification also incorporating the retiming of the voice announcement to be made more accurately at station stops. The armrests between the seats, too, have not stood the test of time, with all the grey ones on the Central Line trains that remained having been removed. A more durable and heavy duty type of armrest was tried on seven units (91011, 91021, 91073, 91087, 91135, 91287 and 91337) from mid-1996 but these, too, were subsequently removed and it is believed that the trains will be without armrests for the foreseeable future.

The new stock for the Waterloo & City Line comprises two-car trains of 1992 Tube Stock, which were an 'add-on' order to London Underground's 85 eight-car trains. A total of 20 cars were required, with four four-car trains being required for service. Each two-car unit is formed of an 'E' DM and an 'F' NDM, although they are, in most respects, identical to the A-B two-car units on the Central Line. Being then owned by Network SouthEast, the only main visible difference is the application of the Network SouthEast livery. All ten E-F units were delivered to LUL's Ruislip depot in three consignments in March 1993, where they were commissioned for test running prior to being transferred to the Waterloo & City Line. Whilst under test, the trains in their distinctive livery visited most parts of the Central Line, albeit without passengers. These trips were always in eight-car formations, the only time that the DM couplers on these units would be needed under normal service conditions. The interiors are also the same as on the Central Line trains, the only difference being in the style of safety notices and, whilst in Network SouthEast ownership, the lack of route maps.

A 1992 stock train at the Bank end of the Waterloo & City Line. The Network SouthEast unit number has been removed from the cab front. *Capital Transport*

British Rail identified the stock as class 482 and unit numbers were from 501–510. DM 'E' cars are numbered 65501–65510 and NDM 'F' cars 67501–67510. Each are formed into easily identifiable units, 65501–67501 being unit 482.501 and so on up to 65510–67510 (482.510).

Trains were transferred from Ruislip to Waterloo by road and this was done over three weekends – the first trip (four cars) on 7/8th May 1993, another four cars on 27–29th May, with the final 12 going between 8th and 13th June. The first test run from Waterloo to Bank took place on 27th June and driver training commenced the following day. Timetabled 'ghost' running started on 12th July and passengers were carried on the modernised Waterloo & City Line from Monday 19th July 1993, all units being in service at some time throughout the day.

On 1st April 1994 the operation of the Waterloo & City Line was taken over by London Underground. Being the Easter weekend, the line was closed for staff training and familiarisation, reopening under its new owners on Tuesday 5th April. The line is part of the Central Line Business Unit, which provides the operational and maintenance staff. The former NSE 'class', 'flash' and 'unit' numbers have since been removed, although they remain on the inner end NDM 'F' cars. These trains, too, suffered with set number and destination display problems and from October 1995 until February 1996 card train set numbers were carried in the front cab door. From 8th July 1996, 'Correct Side Door Enable' equipment was commissioned on the line. This equipment, also operational on the Central Line (along with the Piccadilly, Circle, Hammersmith & City and Metropolitan lines) is designed to prevent passenger doors being opened on the wrong side of the trains at stations. Despite now being in LUL ownership, the Waterloo & City Line's trains of 1992 Tube Stock remain in NSE livery and are likely to do so for the foreseeable future.

Underground roundels have been added to the sides of the former class 482 units to cover the NSE name. Otherwise the livery is unchanged from NSE days. *Capital Transport*

The first train of 1995 stock for the Northern Line is seen at Hampstead prior to entering service. Later units were delivered with slightly deeper cab door windows. *London Underground Ltd*

Facing page: A train of 1996 stock near West Ham. *Brian Morrison*

1995 & 1996 TUBE STOCKS

The 1995 and 1996 Tube Stocks are almost identical to each other in appearance but there are equipment differences between each type. All trains are being assembled by GEC Alsthom Metro-Cammell Ltd at Washwood Heath, Birmingham. The car body shells are being built in Barcelona, the doors in Canada and the bogies by ACR at Le Creusot in France.

One main difference between the previous build of stock (the 1992 stock for the Central Line) is in the origins for the Jubilee Line trains, with a once proposed scheme for them to be a mix of 1983 stock, refurbished and converted to run with newly-built cars to make up the 59 trains required. To make all the cars have a similar look, the saloon windows on the 1996 (and 1995 stock) have standard-designed double-width saloon windows of the same height as on the 1983 stock.

The 59 six-car trains of 1996 Tube Stock are being built exclusively for the Jubilee Line, to operate the complete service on that line, which is being extended from Green

Park to Stratford via Waterloo, London Bridge and the Docklands area of Canary Wharf and North Greenwich. The maintenance of the trains will be undertaken at the purpose-built new depot at Stratford Market, although some trains will continue to be stabled at Neasden depot and Stanmore sidings. The first train was delivered to Ruislip depot on 18th July 1996 and press launch trips took place on the Jubilee Line Extension test tracks near Stratford on 9th January 1997 and between Stanmore and Wembley Park on the existing line on 14th February 1997. The new trains are being introduced onto the existing Jubilee Line between Stanmore and Charing Cross, replacing the 1983 stock on a 'one-for-one' basis, while the balance of new trains will be transferred to Stratford Market depot in readiness for the opening of the extension in 1998.

The trains are formed into three-car M-T-UNDM units, using the standard 'A' end (even numbers) and 'D' end (odd numbers) system of identification. They are finished in London Underground's Corporate livery. Like the 1992 Tube Stock on the Central Line, the cars are built to the standard tube profile by welding full-length longitudinal aluminium extrusions and thus the sliding doors are on the exterior of the car body. The front cab door incorporates pull-down detrainment steps, should it be necessary to detrain passengers onto the track. Illumination for this is provided by two lights in the head/tail light group below the driving cab windows. The LCD destination indicator and train set number are located above the front cab door. The order includes 20 de-icing trailers in 'A'-end units.

Inside, all seats are longitudinal, there being seats for 32 passengers in DM cars and 34 each in trailer and UNDM cars. Around the door areas in the centre saloon section, moquette-covered perch seats are provided, along with those at the car ends on either side of the communicating door. The resultant larger interior spaces makes it possible to accommodate wheelchairs. For the visually impaired, bright yellow grab rails and poles have been used throughout. The interior colour scheme is a pleasing finish of cream with bright blue uprights around the doorway areas and purple armrests. In addition to the now standard public address equipment, passenger announcements can be made, either automatically or initiated by the Train Operator. The operation of the emergency pull-down alarm handles for passengers provides a talk-back facility with the Train Operator. Some of the emergency handles are located at a lower position for use by disabled passengers.

In the Train Operator's cab, a combined traction/brake controller with 'deadman' device is incorporated within the arm of the Train Operator's adjustable seat. A display for the Train Operator of the Train Management System is provided on the right-hand side of the cab.

The 1996 stock is powered by four frame-mounted 3-phase induction motors per motor car. All four motors are fed from a single voltage-sourced inverter, derived from one of those used on main line class 465 Networker trains. The system is capable of regenerative braking and carries a fully rated dynamic brake resistor and thus regenerative, rheostatic and friction braking are all available. Electrical loads on the trains are fed at either 630V d.c. in the case of traction drives and saloon heating, 240V a.c. for saloon ventilation and 52V d.c. for the train's control functions and all other loads. The bogies are conventional two-axle, fabricated H-frames, fitted with rubber suspension.

Should passenger traffic on the Jubilee Line exceed current estimates, provision has been made for an additional trailer to be inserted in each 'D' end unit, between the UNDM and existing trailer. If built, these cars will be numbered 96601–96717, odd numbers only.

The 1995 Tube Stock is being built by and will be maintained by GEC Alsthom Metro-Cammell Ltd, under a private finance initiative, and will be leased to London Underground for 25 years, to provide the service on the Northern Line. Until all the new trains are available, GEC Alsthom are also maintaining the existing stock on the Northern Line until its withdrawal.

The first train of 1995 Tube Stock was delivered to Ruislip depot on 20th December 1996. Whilst the three-car units are nominally regarded as 'A' or 'D' end units and are numbered appropriately, all units are completely reversible so that a train may comprise two units of one type. This is necessary because the Kennington loop on the Northern Line results in trains becoming 'turned' during the course of their duty.

The trains will initially be driven under manual conditions by a Train Operator but will have the facility to permit ATP and ATO to be equipped at a later date. Whilst the Jubilee and Northern Line trains are quite similar, those for the Northern Line incorporate tip-up seats by the door stand-backs in the centre section of the saloon, a different seating moquette and black armrests. Whereas the cab door on Jubilee Line stock can open downwards for emergency detrainment, more conventional arrangements apply in the Northern Line version. All trains will have in-car video recording equipment. Rubber inter-car gap protectors have been provided at the car ends, to prevent passengers falling between cars. Unlike other tube stock built in the 1990s, whose five-digit numbers all begin with '9', the 1995 Tube Stock breaks tradition by beginning with '5'. In the order of 106 six-car trains, there will be 26 de-icing trailers, equally split between 'A' and 'D' units.

The controls, indications and twin platform CCTV monitors are situated directly in the Train Operator's line of sight, while the a.c. traction package uses Insulated Gate Bi-polar Transistor technology instead of GTO thyristors as on the Jubilee Line trains.

Interior of 1996 stock DM 96014, looking towards the train operator's cab. Note the perch seats in the centre bay by the doorway area and the lower level passenger alarm for use by passengers in wheelchairs. On the 1995 stock, tip-up seats are fitted in place of the perch seats. *Brian Hardy*

Black, grey and yellow seating moquette is used in the Northern Line's 1995 stock, seen on the first train to be delivered. *London Underground Ltd*

Refurbishment of the A60/62 stock was 75% complete by mid-1997, with 42 trains in service. A60 DM 5026 is at the rear of a southbound train departing Northwood Hills. *Paul Bradley*

A60/62 STOCK

To coincide with the electrification of the Metropolitan Line from Rickmansworth to Amersham and Chesham and the provision of two additional tracks from Harrow-on-the-Hill to north of Moor Park (Watford South Junction, where the Watford line diverges), new cars to be known as A60 stock were ordered from Cravens Ltd of Sheffield. The stock comprised 124 driving motor cars and 124 trailers, being formed into four car units (M-T-T-M). Numbering is 5000–5123 (DMs) and 6000–6123 (trailers). The first train of A60 stock entered passenger service on 12th June 1961 (units 5004 and 5008). A further order of A stock, almost identical to the first batch, was provided to replace the F and P stocks on the Uxbridge line. This second batch was designated A62 stock and comprised 108 driving motor cars (5124–5231) and 108 trailers (6124–6231). The A62 stock followed on without interruption after the A60 batch and all A stock trains were in service by December 1963. All driving motor cars were provided with automatic couplers, similar to those introduced on the 1960 tube stock, enabling any driving motor car to be coupled to another.

Interior seating is arranged transversely with an off-centre gangway, allowing seats to be arranged in pairs on one side and in groups of three on the other. The DM cars seat 54 passengers and have in addition four tip-up seats at the furthest end from the cab, while trailers seat 58 passengers. Small luggage racks are provided above window level.

Overhauls of unrefurbished A stock ceased in 1996, the last unit being 5024 in September. Most treated at Neasden depot were latterly given smart grey roofs as seen on this example arriving at Wembley Park. *Brian Hardy*

A60 and A62 stock units were interchangeable until converted for one-person operation (OPO), and operated in eight-car formations of two four-car units. The practice of operating single four-car units in off-peak times was discontinued in 1981. However, the Chalfont-Chesham shuttle service is operated by a single unit and four-car trains have operated on the East London Line from June 1977 until the end of April 1985 and from May 1987 until 24th March 1995, when the line closed for tunnel refurbishment. A stock will return to the East London Line in 1998 when it re-opens.

The versatility of the A stock fleet was demonstrated in 1981, when 'D' end DM 5043 temporarily replaced 'A' DM 5056, the latter being under repair. Compared to some other stocks, changes to unit formations have been few, but following a collision at Kilburn in December 1984, four cars salvaged from it (5028–6028–6117–5117) were formed into one unit in June 1985 and renumbered 5232–6232–6233–5233 in August 1985. DM 5008 replaced 5034 in July 1985, each being renumbered with the (new) 5008 and 5009 being stored damaged, along with trailers 6008 and 6009.

In the meantime, plans were drawn up to convert and adapt the A60/62 stock for One-Person Operation. This would involve extensive alterations, but would be more financially viable than ordering new stock and scrapping trains that still had some 15–20 years operational life left. A total of 56 of the original 58 eight-car trains remained and were thus converted to OPO between April 1985 and September 1986, some at Ruislip depot, but mostly at Acton Works. It was this conversion that reduced the flexibility of the stock, as the fleet was then divided into 44 'A' end units, 44 'D'

Interior views of A stock in unrefurbished and refurbished condition. The latter presents a modern and bright finish, with windows cut into the trailing ends of the cars.
Alan Kybird and Capital Transport

end units and 24 double-ended units. A total of 88 DMs were thus relegated to the middle of train formations and the expense of high-intensity headlights, door controls and missile-proof windscreens on those cars was then thus avoided. From OPO conversion, coupling was strictly 'A' to 'D', with the relevant end letters being applied to all DM ends. These were colour-coded red and green, and only green 'A' and 'D' ends could be coupled together for service. The first converted train in crew-operated mode was in service from 19th November 1985 (units 5038 and 5227), while OPO on the Metropolitan Line commenced on 29th September 1986.

These views of middle DM cars on A stock show the retention of their twin headlamps on OPO conversion and the fitting of high-intensity headlights upon refurbishment. *Brian Hardy*

Not included in the OPO conversion programme were stored cars 5008 (ex-5034), 5009, 6008, 6009, 6029, 6116 and 6171, along with unit 5036–6036–6037–5037 which had been cannibalised for spares and hand not run in service since July 1977. In addition, cars 5170, 6170, 5029, 5116 and 5171 were scrapped between 1981 and 1987.

In 1986 trailer 6036 was converted at Acton Works into a 'Rail Treatment Car', to dispense Sandite (an adhesion improver) on running rails. This is particularly necessary north of Rickmansworth on the Metropolitan Line each autumn in the leaf-fall season. The converted car was formed into a four-car double-ended unit of A stock (making five cars in all) and underwent tests in the autumn of 1986. Tests were successful and in each autumn the car works during the leaf-fall period inserted into various double-ended units. Between the 1986 experiments and its first regular annual use in 1987, the body of car 6036 was repainted off white and its roof in Metropolitan Line maroon.

The seven units that work the East London Line were the first members of A stock in passenger service to be exterior painted. Unit 5066 was completed first at Ruislip in November 1988 in off-white with blue doors, grey roofs and red cab ends. The other six units followed in 1989–90 but these were painted by Vic Berry of Leicester where they were taken by road from and to Ruislip (initially) and (later) Neasden. Units 5058, 5062, 5064 and 5232 were painted similarly to 5066 (with minor differences), while unit 5056 was painted in off-white below waist level and blue above waist level, but still with red cab ends and grey roof. The last unit to be painted (5122) was in 'red doors' livery – off-white with blue 'skirt', red doors and cab ends but with a white roof. This is the livery that is now used on all painting schemes for passenger stock, except that the roof colour is grey. As the A stock for the East London Line is maintained at Neasden, it was not uncommon for these painted units to work on the Metropolitan Line to Uxbridge, Watford and Amersham, which indeed happened daily after the East London Line closed for modernisation in March 1995.

Only the first six units of A60 stock were delivered with black roofs and those were given grey roofs by 1967. However, the wearing off of the roof paint has meant that DM 5034 (originally 5008) now shows its roof in original condition. It is seen entering Moor Park. *Brian Hardy*

In preparation to the intended refurbishment of A stock, two cars (5132 and 6132) were selected for trials. The work was done by Metro-Cammell in 1989 and the exteriors were painted in the same style as unit 5056. Inside trailer 6132, panelling and seating moquette were replaced and new flooring fitted. More substantial changes were made to the inside of 5132 and both cars were given pull-down hopper windows. It was decided, however, that further trials were required and the complete four-car unit (5132–6132–6133–5133) returned to Metro-Cammell in February 1990. The four-car unit was delivered back to Neasden in early June 1990 and the exterior was painted into 'red doors' livery with grey roof. Inside, the colour scheme was cream and pale pink with a dark grey area around ankle level. Floor-to-ceiling poles were fitted and these along with other grab poles were finished in a pale blue. The old draught screens to the ceilings were replaced by those finishing at head height only. New vandal-resistant car seats were individually shaped and a new moquette was used. All four cars were given hopper windows in place of the former tilting quarter lights. The unit re-entered service on 8th August 1990.

To provide additional stock to cover for the A stock refurbishment programme, eight of the damaged and almost derelict A60 stock cars (5008–6008–6009–5009 and 5036–6116–6037–5037) have been repaired and reinstated to operational condition, forming two double-ended four-car units. To that end they were taken to BREL Derby by road in August 1990. Lack of funding initially prevented the refurbishment programme going ahead in 1991 and the repair of the eight derelict cars took longer than anticipated. However, cars 5036, 5037, 6037 and 6116 returned from ABB to Neasden in August 1992 in unrefurbished condition. By this time, the go-ahead had been given to refurbish the A stock and the interior fittings for 5036–6116–6037–5037 were obtained from unit 5173 which had been transferred to ABB in August 1992 to be part of the first refurbished eight-car train (along with 5008–6008–6009–5009). Cars 5036, 6037 and 5037 were renumbered (respectively) 5116, 6117 and 5117 in April 1993 and the complete four-car unit (5116–6116–6117–5117) re-entered service on 7th May 1993.

Sandite trailer 6036 has been refurbished and painted in Corporate livery, having previously served as a guinea pig for A stock roof and car body painting. It now matches its partners when it works in a four-car unit on leaf-clearing duties each autumn. *Les Collings*

Since 1986, DM 5209 has taken the place of collision-damaged 5121 and in March 1993 DM 5209 was renumbered 5121 after being converted into a double-ended DM. The other three cars of the unit (5208–6208–6209) had been stored since OPO conversion in 1986 and in August 1992 DM 5208 replaced 5218 and was accordingly renumbered. The original 5218, 5121, trailers 6208 and 6209 and 6029 and 6171 were scrapped in 1994. The total stock for the Metropolitan Line (and East London Line), in June 1997, comprises 44 'A' end units, 43 'D' end units and 26 double-ended units, making 56½ eight-car trains.

The refurbishment of A stock eventually commenced in 1992, the first train comprising ex-derelict unit 5008–6008–6009–5009 which became double-ended de-icing unit 5234–6234–6235–5235, along with 5172–6172–6173–5173. The complete train returned to Neasden on 23rd April 1994, entering service on the Metropolitan Line on 22nd September 1994. To date, 42 refurbished trains have been commissioned for service, including the 'Sandite' trailer which works each autumn in a four-car double-ended unit. Two single 'A'-end units 5000 and 5004 have been fitted with de-icing equipment on refurbishment.

Refurbished trains are fitted with Correct Side Door Enable equipment, which was introduced on the Metropolitan Line on 25th November 1996. They are painted in LUL Corporate 'red doors' livery. The ventilator over the destination blind has been removed and the whistle re-positioned in the dome of the grey roof. Inside, the traditional maple wood flooring has been replaced by rubber matting and a new ceiling design incorporates new lighting. The gravity tilting opening quarter lights have been replaced by spring hopper windows. Windows have been fitted at the trailing ends of DM cars and both ends of trailers for added passenger security. The A stock was the last of LUL's trains to retain passenger alarm handles which, when operated, stopped the train. Refurbished trains have the now standard system where trains can continue to the next station if the alarm is operated. Metropolitan Line coloured grab poles have replaced and supplemented the former grab handles and interior panelling is off-white with a pale pink around the window areas.

C69 and C77 stock in refurbished condition are now indistinguishable. A train arrives at Barking which, until September 1996, was served by the Hammersmith & City Line in peak hours only. *Brian Hardy*

C69/77 STOCK

The Circle and Hammersmith & City Lines were operated by six-car trains of converted CO and CP stock until the delivery of the C69 stock. The letter 'C' indicates 'Circle' – there has been no B stock in modern times. The first train of C69 stock entered service on 28th September 1970 (units 5522, 5523 and 5524) and all were in service by December 1971.

The new stock comprised 106 driving motor cars (5501–5606) and 106 trailers (6501–6606), formed into two-car semi-permanently coupled units (M-T). All units were identical and at the outer ends of each a fully-automatic reversible coupler was fitted. The six-cars for each train could therefore be formed M-T+T-M+T-M or M-T+M-T+T-M.

Each car has four sets of double passenger doors on each side, with seating capacity reduced in consequence to 32. On the lines which the stock operates, the majority of passenger journeys are of short distances and so the additional doors were introduced to allow increased speed in boarding and alighting in busy periods. Each pair of doors is separated by double-glazed car windows. On the driving motor cars the cab door is also air operated, being independently controlled. The door control panels are located in the cab, as on the O stock previously working on the Hammersmith & City Line. Public address is fitted to enable the driver to make announcements to the passengers. A 'selective close' facility is provided at terminal stations in cold weather.

When new, 14 trailers (6543–6556) were fitted with de-icing equipment, but three of these have since been decommissioned (6554–6556). Air metacone suspension was provided on the trains from new, following trials on A62 stock DM car 5218. Rheostatic braking as on 1967 stock is also fitted. Provision was also made in the design for the trains to be converted to One-Person Operation and all cars have since been modified. Ceiling-mounted fans were located at each door position for heating, being thermostatically controlled. A hydraulic parking brake was fitted in each DM cab and all cars had illuminated interior advertisement panels on the bulkhead dividing the saloon from the doorway area.

To replace the six-car trains of CO/CP stock operating the Wimbledon to Edgware Road section of the District Line, eleven six-car trains of C77 stock were ordered from Metro-Cammell. Delivery commenced in July 1977. The cars are similar to the C69 stock and likewise are formed into two-car reversible units (M-T) with an automatic coupler at each outer end. In consequence, the maintenance of C77 stock trains is carried out at Hammersmith depot. The first train of C77 stock entered service on the Hammersmith & City Line on 12th December 1977 (units 5701, 5702 and 5703).

Interior of refurbished C stock. It continues to seat 32 passengers but now longitudinally in pairs separated by armrests. *Brian Hardy*

The C77 stock order included one extra DM car. This was numbered 5585 and replaced the original which was bomb-damaged beyond repair at West Ham in March 1976. Its trailer, 6585, was less severely damaged and was repaired at Acton Works. Interior car heaters on C77 stock initially comprised panels below the draught screen at floor level but during 1979/80 additional heaters were fitted up to draught screen level, covered with a blue aerowalk material.

The intention to operate the C stock as One-Person Operated trains was frustrated by protracted negotiations between management and unions and it was not until 26th March 1984 that OPO was introduced on the Hammersmith & City Line. The Circle Line followed suit from 22nd October 1984 and the Wimbledon-Edgware Road section of the District Line (along with the District main line) from 4th November 1985.

The C stock then entered a period of relative stability until consideration was given to refurbishing it. C77/69 stock unit 5585–6585 was chosen as the prototype and work was undertaken at BREL, Derby in 1989. The exterior of both cars was painted blue above waist level and white beneath, with a red driving cab front and grey roof. Both cars had the maple wood flooring replaced by light grey grooved moulded flooring and the trailing ends were fitted with windows to improve visibility between cars, thus enhancing passenger security. Other changes included the fitting of a spring-applied parking brake. Inside DM 5585 new seating moquette and suspended rectangular yellow grab rails for standing passengers were fitted. More substantial changes were made to trailer 6585, where the transverse seats were replaced by longitudinal seating with the loss of six seat positions. The fitting of a shunting control cabinet to the uncoupling end of 6585 caused the loss of one further seat and thus the number of seats in this car was reduced from 32 to 25, although standing capacity was greatly increased. The ceiling bulkheads in 6585 were redesigned, eliminating the illuminated advertisement positions, while the draught screens were reduced in size – the grab poles and glass slanted inwards towards the body above waist level.

Having been displayed to the public, the unit entered service on 22nd November 1989. The success of the refurbishment led to a contract being awarded to RFS Industries of Doncaster for the C69 and C77 stock fleet to be refurbished and painted, the first units being transferred to RFS in 1990. The external finish is in the LUL 'red doors' corporate livery and the internal finish is from a design by Cre'active. The interiors of all cars retain their 32 seat capacity, but all seats are now longitudinal and in pairs separated by armrests. This seating arrangement allows a greater area for standing passengers and makes it even harder (if not impossible) for the undesirables to put their feet on the opposite seats. Additionally, twin yellow grab rails run the length of the car at head height in place of strap hangers. Along the roof line, slots have been cut into the car roof to expel air, should fans be fitted at a later date (trailer 6513 was fitted with air cooling equipment in refurbished condition but this has now been removed, pending any further decisions on this). The refurbishment also included replacing the air suspension using the rubber 'blobs' (as on D stock), the provision of new bogies and spring-applied parking brakes. Trailer 6527, which had grilles in the ventilation slots above the car windows, was converted to standard. Trailer 6567, however, retains its tinted glass car windows, a legacy of interior cooling trials in the mid-1970s.

The last refurbished train of C stock returned to LUL on 9th April 1994, re-entering service on 5th May 1994. On a refurbished C69 or C77 stock train, it is no longer possible to distinguish between the two types in appearance.

One unit of C69 stock was not included for refurbishment, being 5606–6606 which had been fitted with experimental traction equipment by Kiepe in 1974. In need of replacement and requiring extensive modification to convert it back to standard, it was declared withdrawn, having been taken out of service in January 1991. In May 1993 it was taken to RFS Doncaster, ultimately for disposal.

Since the last edition of this handbook, all D stock has received a package of engineering modifications. Whilst most are not seen by the public, one which is visible is the relocation of the train whistle above the left-hand cab window, as illustrated on this eastbound train arriving at Chiswick Park. *Capital Transport*

D STOCK

The D stock comprises 75 trains which replaced the bulk of the District Line's CO/CP and R stocks between 1980 and 1983. Each train is composed of six cars, but each car is about 60ft long and a train of D stock is approximately the same length as the seven-car train it replaced. The train formation is as used for the 1973 tube stock on the Piccadilly Line. Most trains have two single-cab units with automatic couplers on the middle UNDM cars, and 65 east and 65 west facing single cab units were built. Twenty double-cab units with automatic couplers at each driving end were also built and these units were the first type to be delivered. D stock is numbered 7000–7129 (DMs), 7500–7539 (DMs with automatic couplers), 8000–8129 (UNDMs), 17000–17129 (trailers) and even numbers only from 17500–17538 (trailers used in double-cab units).

Each of the four passenger doorways on each side of the car is 3ft 6ins wide, 1ft less than each double doorway on CO/CP and R stocks. A single leaf sliding door is fitted at each opening, a design feature now considered to have been a mistake. Draught screens are set back from the door openings by about 8ins. DM cars seat 44, trailers and UNDMs seat 48. One transverse seat bay on each side of the car is provided in the centre section of all cars – all other seats are longitudinal.

Passenger door control was reintroduced with this stock, a facility that had not been provided since the second world war. Each doorway has three 'passenger open' buttons, two inside and one outside. The 'selective close' facility for passenger comfort is provided as on C69/77 stock and a new 'selective reopen' facility is installed whereby it is possible to reopen only the doors on those cars where they have failed to close properly. The door controls are located in the driving cabs.

To improve riding quality, a new type of bogie was tested on A62 stock car 5218 for use on D stock. This incorporated suspension using two hemispherical rubber cushions supporting a coil spring and replaced an earlier plan to use air bags. The motors and wheel sets are interchangeable with those on 1973 tube stock, though little interchange has occurred. Fans are installed in the car ceilings for ventilation and 'Pyro-bar' type car heaters are also installed.

Interior of a D stock car, showing at the end the brown-painted communicating doors that replaced the orange doors upon repainting. Refurbishment of this stock has been delayed by cuts in the Underground's financial support. *Brian Hardy*

A new type of driver's control handle is incorporated and operates in the 'fore' and 'aft' positions. This type of controller was tried out on the experimental 1935 tube stock, but the handle has to be kept twisted while the train is in motion (this position being equivalent to the dead man's handle) and moved forward for motoring and back for braking. The driver's seat is a swivelling design instead of a 'pull down' and adjusts up and down as well as forwards and backwards. As on the 1973 Tube Stock, a fault-finding Train Equipment Panel (TEP) is provided (with modifications) as are air-operated sliding cab doors. A spring-applied parking brake is fitted instead of the hydraulic type fitted to previous stocks. Only one compressor is fitted on each single-cab unit, but the double-cab units have two. The first 25 trailers in west end single-cab units (17000/2/4 up to 17048) have been equipped with de-icing equipment.

The first unit of D stock was delivered on 29th June 1979 to Ruislip depot and was transferred to Ealing Common for commissioning on the same day. The commissioning of all D stock was undertaken at Ealing Common, and the first train entered service on Monday 28th January 1980 formed of cars 7532–17532–7533 + 7528–17528–7529.

Unit 8043–17043–7043, which was delivered in November 1980, is fitted with Knorr-Bremse experimental braking equipment, which is of German manufacture. Having been used on extensive tests, it entered service in April 1981. Unit 7080–17080–8080, delivered in October 1981, is fitted with Westinghouse Analogue braking.

In order to assist disabled passengers, one door on each side of each car was fitted with a grab handle. All units from 7082–17082–8082 onwards were fitted with them at Metro-Cammell and those in service before unit 7082 were modified at Ealing Common. These handles had to be removed in 1990 owing to misuse by the hooligan element of society.

DM 7108 of unit 7108–17108–8108 was delivered in June 1982 with experimental ventilation equipment, including grilles over the car windows, pull-down quarter lights, except at door pockets and additional slots for expelled air on the car roof. Following the testing of this equipment it was decided that all D stock trains should be modified similarly, but without the grilles above the windows. The prototype unit returned to Metro-Cammell in October 1982, being modified and returned with the last unit of D stock (8129–17129–7129) on 29th June 1983 exactly four years from the delivery of the very first unit. The 20 double-cab units of D stock were modified at Acton Works between March 1983 and June 1984, whereas the single-cab units were returned to Metro-Cammell at Birmingham in pairs from March 1983, the last to be received back in modified condition being units 7080 and 7059 in January 1985. DM 7108 remains distinguishable as the prototype in that the grilles over the car windows have been panelled over.

With service reductions having taken place on most Underground lines from December 1982 and ventilation modifications being completed in January 1985, there was ample spare D stock available to provide the service on the East London Line, allowing displaced A60/62 stock to form a float for OPO conversion. Double-cab units of D stock took over on the East London Line from 27th April 1985, initially as crew-operated trains, but OPO from 13th May 1985. The upturn of traffic caused subsequent need to increase the District Line service and with the A stock OPO conversion completed, the latter returned to the East London Line in May 1987, the complete D stock fleet now operating on the District main line.

Engineering modifications to the D stock took place between 1994 and 1996. The only visible differences were with the train whistle, which was moved above the left front cab window, and a new cab door between the saloon and driver's cab. During these modifications Train Monitoring System equipment replaced the original TEPs and Correct Side Door Enable equipment was fitted. All modifications were completed by December 1996.

With the D stock now approaching half of its operational life, a proposal for refurbishment was made but deferred because of financial constraints.

Battery locomotive L51 reverses in platform No. 1 at Amersham on a test train comprising Metro-politan electric locomotive No. 12 'Sarah Siddons' and two brake vans. These two vehicles comprise B558 in maroon and an acquired ex-BR brake van in red. This latter vehicle has been nominally allocated the number B586. *Fred Ivey*

ENGINEERS' TRAINS

The vehicles of London Underground's service stock fleet are maintained and operated by the 'Transplant' business unit of LUL. The mainstay of London Underground's service stock locomotives are 29 battery locomotives built between 1964 and 1974. The 13 Metro-Cammell 1964-built locomotives (L20–32) included eight for the Victoria Line, L25–32 originally having ATO equipment fitted, the others replacing steam locomotives. As with previous battery locomotives, although the bodies were built new, the traction motors, bogies and compressors were acquired from withdrawn stock. A further batch of five locomotives (L15–19) was built by Metro-Cammell in 1970–71 and provided the additional locomotives needed for the construction of the original section of the Jubilee Line. An additional eleven locomotives (L44–54) were built by BREL at Doncaster in 1973–74, allowing some older machines to be withdrawn and providing new locomotives for the construction of the Heathrow extension of the Piccadilly Line. This last mentioned batch had new instead of second-hand bogies.

L44 is one of seven battery locomotives of 1973 vintage that have
been repainted into blue livery.
This photograph, taken on 20th
April 1996, was on the occasion of
engineering work south of Neasden, when Metropolitan Line
trains, as seen in the background,
were reversing in the southbound
Jubilee Line platform. *Les Collings*

Since the last edition of this handbook, the Track Recording Train
has lost its distinctive livery, now
being in LUL corporate colours.
The three-car ensemble is seen on
30th June 1996 leaving Barking
heading westbound. The pilot
motors L132 and L133 are now
the only remaining operational
members of 1960 stock in LUL
ownership. *Les Collings*

A heat haze shows above the five-car Tunnel Cleaning Train in Ruislip depot on a hot day in June 1996. *Les Collings*

All locomotives have a cab at each end and are built to tube loading gauge. They are able to operate direct from current or by battery power and are most often used to operate engineers' trains, mainly at night during non-traffic hours. Various modifications have been made to the battery locomotives in recent years, most noticeably the high-intensity headlights, replacement of the hinged buffers by spring buffers, and the fitting of buckeye couplers. More recently, during 1995–96, 18 locomotives have been fitted with ATP equipment for working on the Central Line, while seven of the 1973–74 BREL locomotives have been painted blue – all others are in the standard yellow livery. Following the recent withdrawal of the three remaining 1951–52 Pickering-built locomotives, L50–53 of the 1973–74 batch have been re-fitted at one end with a 'Ward' coupler to operate long rail trains. Of the three older locomotives, L58 and L59 are awaiting scrapping.

A further six locomotives (L62–67) were built by Metro-Cammell in 1985/86, which broke from the traditional design. As well as changes to the front end appearance, which incorporated a cross-walkway in front of the cab windows and a sliding side cab door, Kiepe control equipment was fitted and buckeye coupling was provided from new. All six locomotives are currently out of service, pending a decision on their future.

There are two road/rail 'Unimog' vehicles for shunting use in depots. Being of 1983 vintage (L84) and 1986 (L85) they can normally be found at Ealing Common or Lillie Bridge depots although their use has been as diverse as on the Docklands Light Railway and for the Channel Tunnel construction work.

The other operative locomotives comprise two Ballast Motors and two Pilot Motor cars. The latter pair are the pilot cars for working with the Track Recording car (which was converted by BREL at Derby from a 1973 stock trailer in 1987). The two Ballast Motors, both in yellow livery, are the survivors of 16 converted from withdrawn 1938

The versatility of the Unimog vehicles is shown here in Ruislip depot, with L84 parked away from the track on 30th September 1995. By this time, the vehicle has had a repaint and has acquired the TransPlant name on the cab side. *Les Collings*

Tube Stock between 1973 and 1978. Formed into a paired unit, L150 and L151 have been specially adapted as a Weed Killing train, acquiring its present equipment from Chipman's of Horsham in 1986.

Since the previous edition of this handbook, many surplus vehicles have been withdrawn. These comprise the 1951 battery locomotives, two further ex-1938 stock Ballast Motors, the Sentinel diesel locomotives, the three original diesel electric cranes and their jib carriers, the tube gauging car, along with some flat wagons and rail wagons. The majority have been scrapped, but some have been retained to assist with possible preservation activities. Some have also found use with other operators.

There have, however, been many additions to the fleet. A total of 60 ex-BR 4-axle Turbot wagons were modified by ABB at Crewe, which included air brake modifications, fitting control wiring and complete vehicle overhaul, as well as painting into yellow livery. Being built variously by BR at Shildon and Swindon, and RFS at Doncaster between 1982 and 1988, the modified wagons were delivered to London Underground during January and February 1996. They are used to carry ballast to and from site on major track replacement operations. In 1996, three cable drum wagons were delivered, built by Bombardier, to supplement the existing trio of 1940 vintage. For the construction of the Jubilee Line Extension, 15 general purpose wagons, four bogie well wagons and four 4-wheel cable drum wagons were built by Bombardier and delivered to Neasden in late-1994/early-1995. To haul these wagons, 14 diesel locomotives have been built by Schoma of Germany. The two-axle 32-tonne locomotives have been built to tube loading gauge and are suitable for working in tube tunnels. They are fitted with normal-height buffers and drop-head buckeye couplers. One (No. 5) has been fitted with a Wedgelock coupler for shunting 1996 Tube Stock in Stratford Market depot. All 14 have been given (female) names.

Above: The only operational ballast motor cars of 1938 Tube Stock are a pair in use as the Weed Killing train, all others having been scrapped. The Epping-Ongar single line was visited just prior to closure and the unit is seen in action departing North Weald for Ongar. *Les Collings*

Below: The 22 hopper wagons were built in 1981 by W. H. Davis & Sons. HW210 stands in the southbound 'middle' platform at East Finchley on 23rd March 1996. *Alan Kybird*

Above right: Two of the converted Turbot wagons stand in the eastbound 'fast' (Piccadilly Line) platform at Ravenscourt Park on 27th May 1996 during a major bridge replacement project east of the station. Nearest the camera is SB276. *Fred Ivey*

Right: Used to haul engineers trains in the construction of the Jubilee Line Extension are 14 diesel locomotives built by Schoma of Germany. No. 3, named "Claire", approaches West Ham with a train from Stratford Market depot in August 1996. *Brian Hardy*

Below right: Tamping machine 773 stands in the Permanent Way sidings at the back of Neasden depot. Despite being allocated 'TMM' prefixes, none of the three have yet actually carried these, although they have been in service for some 17 years. *Les Collings*

SAVED FROM SCRAP

London Transport Museum, Covent Garden, London, WC2
The largest and most varied collection of preserved London Underground rolling stock is owned by the London Transport Museum. Much of the collection is housed in the Museum at Covent Garden which opened to the public on 29th March 1980. Some of the exhibits were formerly on display in the London Transport Collection at Syon Park, the predecessor of the London Transport Museum. A complete list of vehicles is given on pages 66 and 67.

The only surviving tube electric sleet locomotive is ESL107, although not in operational condition. It is seen in Ruislip depot on 15th March 1997, having had a recent repaint back into service stock maroon livery. Converted to become a sleet locomotive in 1939, the two motor car halves in fact date back to 1903. *Les Collings*

Below: Interior view of one of the LT Museum's ex-Q38 stock pilot motors, in the process of being restored. *Les Collings*

DM car 16 of 1986 Prototype Tube Stock now belongs to the London Transport Museum, all other cars of the group having been scrapped between August and October 1996. The car is currently stored at Ash Grove garage and is seen on 22nd August 1996 near its new home. *Fred Ivey*

The four-car unit of 1938 Tube Stock that was formerly part of the 'Starlight Express' train now resides in Cockfosters depot, where it is seen on 26th May 1996. The unit is owned by the London Transport Museum. Only DM car 10012 is original, 'D' end DM 11012 was originally 11178. *Robert Sheen*

London Underground Limited

Stored on London Underground metals are a number of vehicles, some of which may ultimately be restored to operational condition. In addition, 12 coaches have been acquired from British Rail and what was Network SouthEast, for use on rail tours or 'Steam on the Met' events. Seven of the coaches were formerly in 4-TC units, the others locomotive-hauled. The complete list of LUL owned vehicles, often referred to as the 'Heritage' fleet, is listed on page 65. None of the vehicles are included in LUL's operational fleet.

Former Isle of Wight motor coach No. 2 (ex-LT 3706 of 1934 vintage) is seen stored in Acton Works, forming part of LUL's 'Heritage' fleet of vehicles. *Les Collings*

A driving trailer of a 4-TC unit leads, with electric locomotive No. 12 'Sarah Siddons' at the rear, approaching Rayners Lane on a railtour on 17th March 1996. Since working on the Underground, the twin roof-mounted warning horns on the unit have had to be moved to below the roof line. *Les Collings*

Alderney Railway Society, Channel Islands.
1938 stock DMs 10177 and 11177. Formerly owned by the North Downs Railway, these two cars were transferred to their new owners in mid-1987.

Bluebell Railway, Sheffield Park, Sussex.
Metropolitan Railway steam stock coaches 368 (1st and 3rd class coach built 1898), 387 (3rd class brake coach built 1898), 394 (3rd class coach built 1900), and 412 (1st and 3rd class coach built 1900). No. 412 was built by Cravens Ltd, Sheffield and the other three by the Ashbury Railway Carriage & Iron Co. The four coaches have a varied history. No. 387 was converted to a 3rd class electric driving motor car in 1907 and became 2761 when owned by the LPTB. No. 394 was converted to a 3rd class control trailer in 1921, becoming No. 6702 with the LPTB. Nos. 368 and 412 were converted to 1st class electric trailers in 1906 and became 9702 and 9705 respectively in LPTB ownership. The four cars were reconverted in 1940 to steam stock for push-pull working on the Chalfont/Chesham shuttle and were further renumbered 512 (2761), 515 (9702), 516 (9705) and 518 (6702). They were withdrawn in 1960 and were acquired by the Bluebell Railway in 1961. The four coaches, having been out of service since 1965–66, are now being restored.

Metropolitan Railway ballast wagon BW4 of 1897 origin, transferred from Neasden depot in June 1982.

Buckinghamshire Railway Centre, Quainton Road, Quainton, Bucks.
Metropolitan Railway class E 0–4–4T steam locomotive No. 1 built by the Metropolitan Railway at Neasden and dating from 1898, renumbered L44 in the service stock fleet by the LPTB in 1938.

London Transport service stock locomotive L99, originally GWR 0–6–0PT loco No. 7715 dating from 1930. This locomotive, along with former L90 from the Birmingham Railway Museum, worked in London Transport livery in May 1993 on the 'Steam on the Met' special trains. L99 also worked the 125th anniversary specials on the District Line on 5th/6th June 1993, between Ealing Broadway and West Kensington.

Ex-Great Western 0–6–0PT locomotive 7715 was sold to the Buckinghamshire Railway Centre after withdrawal from London Transport as L99. More recently it has been painted back into LT colours and has taken part in 'Steam on the Met' events. It is seen at Rickmansworth. *Les Collings*

CP stock DM 54233. This stock was moved to Quainton Road in October 1981 for preservation. After bomb damage during the Second World War, this car was rebuilt using part of Q38 trailer 013167, which had also suffered bomb damage.

In addition, two other cars of similar stock were taken by road from Ruislip depot at the end of June 1984. These were CO DM 53028 and COP trailer 013063. This therefore, makes a complete three-car unit.

Hurst Nelson brake van B557 was acquired by the Centre on the same date as the CP stock car mentioned above.

Five-ton hand-operated crane C619, built in 1914 by Cowan Sheldon, and jib carrier J690. These vehicles were unique in being the only rail vehicles to be owned jointly by the Metropolitan and Great Central Railways. C619 and J690 were normally to be found in Harrow Goods yard. They were withdrawn in 1955 but were not taken to Quainton until May 1970.

LT flat brake wagon FB578, converted in 1950 from four-wheeled flat wagon F327.

LT four-wheeled flat wagon F329, built by Gloucester.

Cobham Bus Museum, Cobham, Surrey.
Cab and small section of passenger saloon of 1938 Tube Stock DM car 11242.

Colne Valley Railway, near Castle Hedingham, Halstead, Essex.
Four wheeled hopper wagon HW421 built in 1951 by Gloucester.

Craven Preservation Group.
1960 Tube Stock three-car unit 3906–4927–3907 and converted trailer 4929, and 1962 Tube Stock four-car unit 1506–2506–9507–1507.

Dart Valley Railway, Totnes, Devon.
Four-wheeled hopper wagon HW418, built 1951 by Gloucester.

Great Eastern Traction, Hardingham, Essex.
Ex-LT Sentinel diesel locomotive DL82.

The three-car train of 1960 prototype Tube Stock remains operational and now belongs to the Craven Preservation Group. It works occasional railtours and special trips, such as this on the Jubilee Line on 18th August 1996, and is seen at Kingsbury. *Les Collings*

Island Line, Isle of Wight

The restricted loading gauge through Ryde tunnels on the Isle of Wight led to withdrawn Pre-1938 Tube stock from London Underground being refurbished for use on the remaining section of the Isle of Wight Railway between Ryde and Shanklin. A total of 43 cars were converted to standard SR third-rail operation, forming six seven-car trains with one spare DM car. Electric services on the Isle of Wight commenced on 20th March 1967.

By 1987 the operational fleet had been reduced to just 27 cars, then formed of five five-car trains and one two-car train. The stock which remained, then varying in age between 53 and 64 years according to the vehicle type, was in need of replacement, as the cost of further life extension was prohibitive. The 1959/62 Tube stock would not be available for some years and the only option (other than closure of the line) was to obtain the remaining cars of 1938 Tube stock from London Underground. The first train of this stock entered service on the Isle of Wight in July 1989 and the last pre-1938 stock ran in February 1990.

The operational fleet of 1938 Tube Stock on the Isle of Wight has been reduced to six two-car units, all other cars being in withdrawn condition. More recently known as the 'Island Line' under the operational arm of South West Trains, the line was taken over by Stagecoach on 13th October 1996.

The rolling stock situation as at 1st June 1997 was as follows:

Class 483 2-Car Units – former LUL numbers in brackets – 20

	FOR SERVICE		WITHDRAWN	
Unit	DM 'A'-end	DM 'D'-end	DM 'A'-end	DM 'D'-end
No.	North	South	North	South
483.002	122 (10221)	225 (11142)	121 (10184)	222 (11221)
483.004	124 (10205)	224 (11205)	123 (10116)	221 (11184)
483.006	126 (10297)	226 (11297)	125 (10142)	223 (11116)
483.007	127 (10291)	227 (11291)	*(10139)	* (11172)
483.008	128 (10255)	228 (11255)		
483.009	129 (10229)	229 (11229)	*Not converted for passenger use	

The operational fleet of 1938 Tube Stock on the Isle of Wight comprises just six two-car units, including 483.008 seen arriving at Ryde St John's Road on 9th May 1995. *Alan Kybird*

Isle of Wight Steam Railway, Haven Street.
Four-wheeled hopper wagons HW435 and HW437, built in 1965 by BR at Shildon.

Keighley & Worth Valley Railway, Yorkshire.
Metropolitan Railway steam stock brake coach 427 (3rd class seven-compartment brake coach built as a 1st class control trailer in 1905), 465 (3rd class nine-compartment coach built 1920), and 509 (1st class seven-compartment coach built 1923). Two of these vehicles (465 and 509) are owned by the Vintage Carriages Trust and are normally on display at Ingrow Museum.

London Transport service stock locomotive L89, originally GWR 0–6–0PT loco No. 5775 dating from 1929.

The Vintage Carriages Trust owns the three ex-Metropolitan Railway 'Dreadnought' coaches. This is seven-compartment first class car 509 built in 1923 and now superbly restored. *Vintage Carriages Trust*

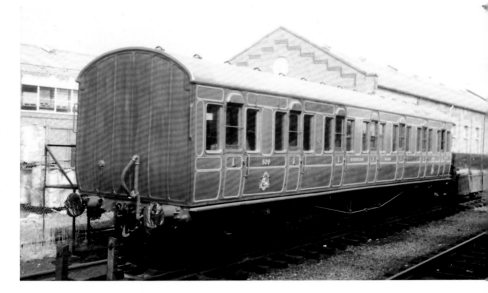

Kent & East Sussex Railway.
In late 1979 and early 1980, restoration was carried out on a coach now numbered as District Railway 100 – a 1st class four-compartment steam stock car dating from around 1865. The coach body was retrieved in two halves which have been joined together and mounted on a modern underframe. Whilst the coach is thus very much a hybrid, it has been superbly restored and saw passenger service from 24th August 1980.

Lavender Line, Isfield, Sussex.
Four-wheel hopper wagons HW402 and HW433, built 1935 and 1951 respectively by Gloucester.

London Underground Railway Society.
The bodies of City & South London Railway loco-hauled coaches 135 (dating from 1902) and 163 (dating from 1907).

District Line Q35 stock trailer 08063, formerly N class trailer (1st and 3rd class) 8063 built in 1935. It was renumbered in 1950 when converted to air-door operation.

The two surviving R stock motor cars from the District Line are now located at Mangapps farm at Burnham-on-Crouch. These comprise R38 DM 22624 in red livery (but with incorrect white car numbers and roundels) and R49 DM 21147 (minus its bogies) painted white. The former is shown here. *Les Collings*

Mangapps Farm Railway, near Burnham-on-Crouch, Essex.
District Line R38 motor car 22624 (originally Q38 trailer 014178, converted 1950) and R49 motor car 21147. The latter was one of just six R49 aluminium DMs, being one of three painted.

Museum of London.
Steam Crane C621, built by Thomas Smith & Sons, 1935, second-hand ex-McAlpine in 1958.

Nene Valley Railway, Peterborough.
Ex-LT Sentinel diesel locomotive DL83.

North Norfolk Railway, Sheringham.
Four-wheeled hopper wagons HW426 and HW429, built in 1951 by Gloucester.

North Woolwich Old Station Railway Museum.
CP stock DM 54256, moved from Ruislip depot by road in November 1982. Now unlikely to be restored due to vandalism on site at North Woolwich.

Pilot Holdings, Ongar, Essex.
1962 Tube Stock units 1490–2490–9491–1491 and 1616–2616–9617–1617 were transferred to Ongar in October 1996, pending decisions to be made on the operation of the line for the future.

The ex-London Underground vehicles that belonged to the North Downs Steam Railway have all been moved to the Spa Valley Railway at Tunbridge Wells. These include the former T stock sleet two-coach unit of which ESL118B is seen. *Alan Kybird*

Rutland Railway Museum, Cottesmore.

Ex-LT Sentinel diesel locomotive DL81 acquired in 1994.

Weighing machine adjustment van TV751 (ex Metropolitan Railway No. 7) was disposed of by the LPTB in 1944. It was purchased in 1981 from British Steel at Kettering.

Spa Valley Railway, Tunbridge Wells, Kent.

Former T Stock DMs 2758 and 2749 (originally 258 and 249, latterly ESL118A/B respectively).

Hurst Nelson brake van B560 of 1935 (this replaced B556, which was damaged by fire and is now rebuilt as a box van).

Ex-LT diesel electric crane DEC622, built 1964 by Taylor & Hubbard, and jib carrier JC689. The latter is a former 1925 vintage flat wagon, converted to a jib carrier in 1952.

Ex-LT flat wagon F397 built in 1965 by Gloucester.

Severn Valley Railway, Bridgnorth, Shropshire.

London Transport service stock steam locomotive L95, originally GWR 0–6–0PT 5764, and Lining Machine PTL764.

Southern Steam Trust, Swanage.

Plasser Theurer VKR05 Tamping Machine PBT762, built in 1966.

Other Stock:

There are a small number of other ex-LUL vehicles in private ownership and these are excluded from the lists above to respect owners' wishes for anonymity. There are also a number of other non-passenger vehicles which have been sold for disposal by London Underground and have since been refurbished for use by other operators.

Details of any vehicles not included here would be welcomed by the author, via the publisher.

PRESERVED LIST – LONDON UNDERGROUND

No.	Details
2	DM car (ex-LT 3706) built 1934 by Metro-Cammell, ex Isle of Wight.
7	DM car (ex-LT 3209) built 1931 by Metro-Cammell, ex Isle of Wight.
L11	Double-ended ex-Acton Works shunting locomotive (ex–3080/3109) built 1931 by Metro-Cammell and converted 1964.
12	Metropolitan Railway electric locomotive, named 'Sarah Siddons' and built 1922 by Metropolitan Vickers.
44	Trailer car (ex-LT 7281) built 1923 by Cammell Laird, ex Isle of Wight.
DT81 DT82 DT83	Diesel tenders from Sentinel diesel locomotives.
L130	Ex Tube Stock pilot motor car, converted 1967, ex 3690 built 1934 by Metro-Cammell.
L135	Ex Tube Stock pilot motor car, converted 1968, ex 3701 built 1934 by Metro-Cammell.
F343	Flat wagon built 1951 by Gloucester.
F362	Flat wagon built 1951 by Gloucester.
F384	Flat wagon built 1965 by BR Ashford.
RW479	Rail wagon built 1950 by Gloucester.
B558	Brake van built 1935 by Hunt Nelson.
B580	Brake van built 1965 by BR Ashford, previously tube stock match wagon.
B583	Brake van built 1965 by BR Ashford, previously surface stock match wagon.
B584	Brake van built 1965 by BR Ashford, previously surface stock match wagon.
B585	Brake van built 1965 by BR Ashford, previously tube stock match wagon.
B586	Brake van built 1962 by BR Ashford, ex-BR B955096
PC850	Ex personnel carrier converted 1966, ex 7061 built 1931 by Birmingham.
PC851	Ex personnel carrier converted 1966, ex 7063 built 1931 by Birmingham.
PC855	Ex personnel carrier converted 1966, ex 7071 built 1931 by Birmingham.
TRC912	Intended track recording car converted 1978, ex 012331 built 1938 by Birmingham.
WPW1000	Ex-diesel generator wagon, well wagon in 1976, built 1937 at Acton Works.

Ex British Rail

No.	Built	Type	Acquired
5458	1969 Derby	TSO	1995
5495	1969 Derby	TSO	1995
5497	1969 Derby	TSO	1995
*70823	1957 Metro-Cammell	TBSK	1992
*70824	1957 Metro-Cammell	TBSK	1992
*70855	1952 Swindon	TFK	1992
*71163	1954 Swindon	TFK	1992
*76297	1955 Ashford/Eastleigh	DTSO	1992
*76298	1957 Ashford/Eastleigh	DTSO	1992
*76322	1955 Ashford/Eastleigh	DTSO	1992
*76324	1957 Ashford/Eastleigh	DTSO	1992
977588	1957 Metro-Cammell	BSK	1988

* Converted to 4-TC stock at York in 1966 (71163 in 1974)

PRESERVED LIST – LT MUSEUM

Vehicles stored and not on display are shown in italics in the following list.

Metropolitan Railway class A 4–4–0T steam locomotive No. 23 was built in 1866 by Beyer Peacock, later becoming service stock locomotive L45. This locomotive was withdrawn in 1948, following which it was restored to 1903 condition and eventually displayed at the Museum of British Transport at Clapham until its closure in 1972, when it moved to the LT Collection at Syon Park. The locomotive also appeared at the Underground Centenary celebrations at Neasden in May 1963.

Brill branch (Wotton Tramway) 0–4–0T steam locomotive No. 807, built in 1872 by Aveling & Porter.

Metropolitan Railway 'Jubilee' steam stock coach dating from between 1887 and 1893 and built by Cravens of Sheffield. It is the intention that this car should be restored for eventual display.

City & South London Railway locomotive-hauled 'padded-cell' coach No. 30 built by the Ashbury Carriage & Iron Co. about 1890. This coach was displayed at the old York Railway Museum from 1938 until its closed in 1973.

Metropolitan Railway milk van No. 3 built in 1896 by Birmingham. It was converted to a breakdown van by the LPTB and renumbered BDV700. It was restored to original condition for the Underground Centenary in May 1963.

Metropolitan Railway 10-ton Ballast Wagon BW214 of 1897 origin. This was one of two wagons that survived at Neasden until acquired by the Museum in 1982.

Metropolitan Railway steam stock 2nd class coach No. 400 dating from 1900 and built by the Metropolitan Railway at their Neasden Works. It was converted from steam to electric working in 1921 as a 3rd class Control Trailer, renumbered 6703 by the LPTB and reconverted in 1940 to steam stock for push-pull working on the Chesham/Chalfont shuttle service, when it was further renumbered 519. After withdrawal in 1960 it was stored at Clay Cross from 1962 and later at Preston Park, Brighton. In July 1976 the coach returned to London Transport for restoration at Ruislip depot, where work was completed in 1978.

Tube sleet locomotive ESL107. This started life as two separate motor coaches, one built by Metro-Carriage, the other by Birmingham, for the Central London Railway. After withdrawal from service these were converted to become a sleet locomotive in 1939. The LT numbers of ESL107 were 3944 and 3981.

Great Northern, Piccadilly & Brompton Railway tube motor coach No. 51. Built by the Hungarian Railway Carriage & Machinery Works in Raab for the Piccadilly Line, which opened in 1906, it entered service in 1909. It was renumbered by the LER in 1926 and after withdrawal in 1929, became a Ballast Motor in the service stock fleet. However, only the rear end of the car, including to the first window, is preserved, primarily to show the 'gate' end arrangement.

City & South London Railway four-wheeled wagon No. 63. This was one of a batch of 102 such wagons ordered from Gloucester in 1921 to be used during the reconstruction of the C&SLR. The majority were disposed of after the work was complete but No. 63 survived, lying derelict in London Road depot for many years.

Metropolitan Railway electric locomotive No. 5, built by Metropolitan Vickers in 1922 and named 'John Hampden' in 1927. It was withdrawn from service in 1961 and was used as a shunting locomotive at Ealing Common depot and Acton Works until acquired initially for the London Transport Collection in Syon Park.

London Transport Q23 stock driving motor car 4248. It was originally District Railway G class motor coach No. 644 and was built by Gloucester in 1923. It was renumbered 238 by the LER in 1928 and became 4148 in 1933. The number 4248 was applied in 1965 to avoid clashing with one of the numbers intended for the 1967 Victoria Line trailers. All G class motors were originally built with hand-operated doors and were converted to air operation between 1938 and 1940.

London Transport Pre-1938 Tube Stock driving motor car 3327, originally London Electric Railway tube motor coach No. 297 dating from 1927. When withdrawn from service it was displayed in the Science Museum, but in 1996 ownership passed to the LT Museum.

London Transport 1938 Tube Stock motor car 11182, built by Metro-Cammell. This car is restored in Underground train red livery with gold transfers and (dummy) passenger door control push-buttons, typically as they were in the mid-1950s.

The cab end of CP stock DM 54235 (originally P stock Metadyne motor coach 14235, converted and renumbered in 1963) has been converted into a simulator, giving visitors a driver's-eye view of a trip around the Circle Line on film.

Battery locomotive L35, of 1938 vintage and built by Gloucester, withdrawn from service in April 1992.

District Line unpainted aluminium R49 stock driving motor car 22679.

1938 Tube Stock four-car unit 10012–012256–12048–11012. This unit is formed of the remaining four cars of the 'Starlight Express', which was the last train of this stock to be withdrawn from service on the Northern Line in May 1988. Having been stored at Morden, and displayed at the depot's Open Day in November 1990, it has since been transferred to Cockfosters.

Q38 ex-pilot motors L126 and L127 built by Gloucester. These were painted back to red livery in 1990 and were given their former numbers (4416/4417). They are currently at Ealing Common Depot.

District Line Q23 motor coach 4184, built by Gloucester in 1923 as G class motor coach No. 662, renumbered 274 in 1929 and to its present number in 1934. Following withdrawal from the District Line, the car, without its compressors or traction motors, was displayed outside the GRC&W Co.'s factory in Gloucester. Following the closure of the Gloucester factory, the car was put into store and returned to Ealing Common depot on 27th February 1993.

Ultimately to create a working Pre-1938 Tube Stock train, former Pilot Motor cars L131 (1934 Metro-Cammell) and L134 (1927 Metro-Carriage), along with cars 27 (1925 Metro-Carriage) and 49 (1923 Cammell Laird) from the Isle of Wight, have been set aside for this long-term restoration project. Pilot motor cars L131 and L134 were formerly numbered 3693 and 3370 respectively, while the LT numbers of the Isle of Wight cars, which returned to London Underground in October 1990, were 5279 and 7296.

1986 Prototype Tube Stock driving motor car 16, from the 'green' train 'C' built by Metro-Cammell.

City & South London Railway electric locomotive No. 13 dating from about 1890. Originally being housed in the Science Museum as No. 1, it was repainted and transferred to the LT Museum at Covent Garden in 1990 to celebrate the Centenary of the City & South London Railway.

Metropolitan Railway Saloon 1904 coach, acquired by the North Woolwich Old Station Railway Museum in 1985 from the Army at Shoeburyness, passed to the LT Museum for restoration in the summer of 1997.

DEPOTS AND SIDINGS

There are eight main depots which maintain London's Underground rolling stock. The oldest are at Ealing Common, which was completed in 1905 for the electrification of the District Railway, Hammersmith, opened in 1906 for the electrification of the Hammersmith & City Line, and Golders Green, opened in 1907 for the newly-built Charing Cross, Euston & Hampstead Railway and now part of today's Northern Line. Both Hammersmith and Golders Green have access at one end only, the latter site being especially cramped. Northfields was built for the western Piccadilly Line extensions and was opened in 1932. Until 1964 it was home to a handful of District Line trains that then operated to Hounslow West (conversely, Ealing Common depot also had a small number of Piccadilly Line trains until 1964). Neasden Works of the Metropolitan Railway was rebuilt by 1938 to become the major depot for the Metropolitan and Bakerloo lines, the latter being extended from Baker Street to Stanmore in 1939. A new small two-road steam shed was also built at the north end. In anticipation of the Central Line being extended westwards from North Acton to West Ruislip a new depot was built between Ruislip Gardens and West Ruislip. Largely completed in 1939, the Second World War delayed the completion of the project and the depot was put to other uses until 1948, although it was also used to store spare and withdrawn rolling stock. Northumberland Park was built specially for the Victoria Line and was opened in 1968. Not being near an Underground station, a staff platform was built in the depot to enable trains to convey staff to and from the main Victoria Line at Seven Sisters. The most modern depot came into use at Stonebridge Park in 1979 for the Bakerloo Line. The main depot to serve the Jubilee Line and its eastern extension is at Stratford Market. The first train for training purposes arrived by road on 10/11th December 1996 but the depot had already been in use for engineers' vehicles working on the JLE's construction.

There are, in addition, a number of subsidiary and minor depots, some of which provide maintenance facilities, others being purely under-cover stabling accommodation. Built to a similar design and of the same period as Ealing Common and Golders Green, London Road was originally the main depot for the Bakerloo Line. Its extensions and subsequent connections with the rest of the system have seen this depot reduced to a stabling point, with almost all of the original buildings now demolished. Opened in 1913 was the small depot at New Cross on the East London Line, provided when the East London Line was electrified. Queen's Park depot opened in 1915 when the Bakerloo was extended north from Paddington. It comprises two separate buildings, at the south end a two-road four-train shed and a four-road shed north of the station, through which trains for Stonebridge Park and Harrow have to pass in service on the two outer tracks, connecting at the north end with NLR metals. The two centre tracks are used for reversing Queen's Park terminating trains. Stabling accommodation was provided at Edgware in 1924, with the extension north from Golders Green and Hendon. The depot comprises both covered accommodation and stabling sidings. Morden depot was opened in 1926 when what is now the Northern Line was extended from Clapham Common to Morden and, although regarded as a 'minor' depot, it still provides the most trains for service and has many covered roads and extensive sidings. Access is southwards beyond Morden station. Opened in 1932 was Cockfosters depot, having access from both Oakwood and Cockfosters stations. Along with Northfields depot, it replaced the original Piccadilly Line depot at Lillie Bridge (near West Kensington) which subsequently became (and still is) the depot for engineers trains. The former LNER carriage shed at Wellington sidings was adapted to take tube stock, opening as Highgate depot in 1939. Additional sidings were built nearby at the junction of the Alexandra Palace branch (Park Junction) and were known as Highgate

Wood sidings. Hainault depot was built for the (eastern) Central Line extensions, but was put to other uses during the Second World War. It was also home to over 190 cars of Pre-1938 Tube Stock which had to be stored because the New Works extensions were deferred in 1940 until after the war. Hainault depot opened partially in 1947 and was in full use the following year. Access is provided at both ends, via Hainault and Grange Hill stations. Both Hainault and Ruislip depots replaced White City (formerly Wood Lane) depot on the Central Line for maintenance purposes in 1948. The old Wood Lane station layout precluded trains longer than six cars being operated on the Central Line and it was not until White City station replaced it that seven- and eight-car trains could work on the line and into the depot. The present five-road shed at Wembley Park is as rebuilt in 1954, when alterations to the track layout in the area were completed. From then it has been used only by the Metropolitan Line, but hitherto was used by both Metropolitan and Bakerloo trains. On the District Line, a new depot was built east of Upminster station and opened in 1958 and at about the same time nine sidings (for thirteen trains) were opened east of Barking station. These replaced the inadequate facilities at Little Ilford depot (between East Ham and Barking) which was closed and the area used for building East Ham EMU depot for British Railways. The work also coincided with the complete segregation of District Line tracks from those of BR between Campbell Road Junction (east of Bow Road) and Upminster, which had become an operating headache, especially in the Barking area. Stabling accommodation was also provided between on the District Line between Earl's Court and Gloucester Road with access also to and from High Street Kensington. Known as Cromwell Curve depot, there were originally 18 tracks for District Line trains and two for Circle Line trains. When the West London Air Terminal was built above the line, the number of sidings was reduced in 1957 to provide just five six-car and two four-car length sidings, accessible only from the line between Earl's Court and High Street Kensington, unlike the former sidings which had access additionally to and from Gloucester Road. Only the five six-car sidings now remain and these are known as Triangle Sidings.

There are many open-air stabling sidings, which can be summarised thus. On the Metropolitan Line, the sidings at Uxbridge were opened in 1942 for stabling both Metropolitan and Piccadilly Line trains although the latter have not stabled there since January 1991. Additional electrified sidings were provided at Rickmansworth south of the station in 1961 to coincide with the electrification to Amersham. On the Jubilee Line, ten sidings are provided at Stanmore, which were increased from the original seven in January 1977. On the Hammersmith & City and Circle lines, sidings are provided at Edgware Road and Farringdon. There were previously two sidings at Barbican (then called Aldersgate), one of which went after five-car Circle Line trains were eliminated in 1959, but the other survived in use until April 1979. Stabling sidings are provided on the District Line at Parsons Green and Ealing Broadway, both of which had some shorter roads to take uncoupled portions of trains, which practice was abandoned in 1971. Ealing Broadway no longer has any service trains stabled there and the short sidings have been removed, while one extra siding was made available at Parsons Green in December 1958. For the Piccadilly Line extensions in 1932, new sidings were built at Arnos Grove and South Harrow, the latter being on the site of the 1903 car sheds built for the District Railway electrification experiments of the time. The post-war Central Line extensions also gained sidings at the east end, at Woodford in 1947 and Loughton in 1948. Two more were added at the latter in 1963.

There are, in addition, pairs of sidings at the end of some tube lines used to stable trains. These are at Elephant & Castle on the Bakerloo Line, and Brixton and Walthamstow on the Victoria Line. Until April 1989, two Victoria Line trains used to stable overnight at Victoria, but no longer do so.

Mention should now be made of depots that have closed. The short Northern City Line had its depot (latterly just a stabling point) at Drayton Park, which closed in 1975 when British Rail took over the line for the Great Northern inner suburban electrification. The depot buildings were subsequently demolished. In 1982, the few remaining Bakerloo services to and from Watford Junction were withdrawn and trains no longer stabled at Croxley Green depot as they had done from 1917. Croxley Green BR depot was subsequently closed and demolished. Highgate depot, however, eventually had better fortunes. Although rebuilt in 1970, with the general reductions in services requiring fewer trains, it closed on 25th March 1984, although Highgate Wood sidings had been previously closed at the end of 1982. The subsequent upsurge of passenger traffic and the need to provide more trains saw the depot modernised and it reopened in January 1989. Two tracks were set aside until mid-1990 for the safety modifications to the 1956/59 stock to be carried out there. In the same vein, to accommodate additional trains, two extra sidings have been built at Stonebridge Park depot and four at Northumberland Park depot.

In readiness for the new 1995 Tube Stock, all of the depots and stabling points of the Northern Line are undergoing reconstruction. During 1996, some tracks in Morden depot have been lengthened while at Edgware, additional sidings have been built on the south-east side of the station, partly on the site that was originally acquired for the aborted 1935–40 Northern Line extensions. Additional sidings have also been built at High Barnet, while Highgate depot has had its stabling roads doubled in length, while a test track for the new trains is being built. Work continues in 1997 on the reconstruction of Golders Green depot.

In the early days, the individual depots performed most of the overhaul work required on their trains. In the early-1920s, it was decided to concentrate train overhauls in one central location and Acton Works opened for this role in 1922, it being enlarged over the years. Gradually, stock from all lines was taken to Acton Works for overhaul, although for the Hampstead & City (now Northern Line) trains, it was not until 1927 that a connection was opened at King's Cross to enable Acton Works to be reached. Until the Bakerloo Line was extended to Stanmore in 1939, it too had a circuitous route – via Willesden Junction and Earl's Court. Metropolitan stock began overhauls at Acton Works after the formation of the LPTB in 1933.

Modern rolling stock design and technology has reduced the amount of maintenance work required on trains. Thus, for economic reasons, it was decided to transfer overhauls of stock back to selected depots. Acton Works, however, although a shadow of its former self, gained a new Equipment Overhaul Workshop which opened in 1989 and at the end of 1990 a new heavy repair shop was opened on the high level sidings at the Acton Town end of Ealing Common depot. Known as the Depot Engineering Support Unit (DESU) the functions carried out here have recently been transferred back to Acton Works.

As in June 1997 rolling stock overhauls were carried out at the following depots:

Depot	Stock	Line
Neasden	A60/62	Metropolitan
Golders Green	1959	Northern
Northumberland Park	1967	Victoria
Cockfosters	1973	Piccadilly
Stonebridge Park	1972 MkII	Bakerloo

The first cycle of overhauls on District Line D stock was completed in 1996, while budget constraints have caused a suspension of the C69/77 stock heavy overhauls. Work on the 1959 Tube stock is to cease soon, while the 1972 MkI and 1983 Tube stocks face imminent withdrawal.

DEPOT AND SIDING ALLOCATIONS

	BAKERLOO		CENTRAL		NORTHERN	
Main Depots	Stonebridge Park	11	Ruislip	15	Golders Green	16
Subsidiary Depots	Queen's Park	7	Hainault	29	Morden	38
Minor Depots	London Road	10	White City	12	Edgware	11
					Highgate	8
Sidings	Elephant & Castle	2	Loughton	10	High Barnet	7
	Elephant & Castle platforms	1	Woodford	6	Golders Green	4
Totals		31		72		84

	PICCADILLY		VICTORIA		JUBILEE	
Main Depots	Northfields	36	Northumberland Park	33	Neasden	14
Subsidiary Depots	Cockfosters	36				
Minor Depots						
Sidings	Arnos Grove	4	Brixton	2	Stanmore	10
			Walthamstow	2		
Totals		76		37		24

	DISTRICT		CIRCLE/H&C		METROPOLITAN	
Main Depots	Ealing Common	29	Hammersmith	18	Neasden	21†
Subsidiary Depots	Upminster	27				
Minor Depots	Hammersmith	2*			Wembley Park	5
Sidings	Parsons Green	8*	Farringdon	3	Rickmansworth	9
	Barking	5	Barking	7	Uxbridge	7
	Triangle Sidings	5	Edgware Road	1		
Platforms			Edgware Road	2		
Totals		76		31		42

	EAST LONDON		WATERLOO & CITY	
Main Depots	New Cross	5‡	Waterloo	3
Platform			Bank	1
Totals		5		4

* Includes ten C stock trains operating the Edgware Road-Olympia/Wimbledon section of the District Line: two at Hammersmith, five at Triangle sidings (Cromwell Curve) and three at Parsons Green.
† Total for Neasden includes one four-car unit for Chesham shuttle.
‡ East London Line closed until early-1998.

VEHICLES IN STOCK (MID-JUNE 1997)

LINE SUMMARY TOTALS		STOCK SUMMARY TOTALS	
Bakerloo	252	1959	511
Central	680	1960	3
District	450	1962	82
Hammersmith/Circle	276	1967	315
Jubilee	183	1972 MkI	196
Metropolitan	453	1972 MkII	226
Northern	698	1973	523
Piccadilly	523	1983 Batch I	87
Victoria	345	1983 Batch II	99
Waterloo & City	20	1992	680
		1992 (Waterloo & City)	20
Total	3880	1995	18
		1996	108
		Total Tube	2868
1959 Miscellaneous	3		
1960 Miscellaneous	3	A60	244
1962 Miscellaneous	32	A62	209
1983 Withdrawn	3	C69	210
1995 New Northern	18	C77	66
1996 New Jubilee	108	D	450
Total	167	Total Surface:	1179
Grand Total:	**4047**	**Grand Total:**	**4047**

UNIT FORMATIONS

All passenger stock is formed into semi-permanent units of two, three or four cars. These units are coupled to form trains of four, six, seven or eight cars. On the Metropolitan Line (Chesham shuttle) and East London Line (when reopened), single four-car units are used.

Units/cars out of service in line unit formations are shown in italics.

Units/cars out of service and not to run again in service are shown on page 88.

BAKERLOO LINE

1972 MkI & MkII Tube Stock
Four-car 'A' End Units   **Three-car 'D' End Units**

DM 'A' End South Leading	Trailer	Trailer	DM 'D' End North Middle	UNDM 'A' End South Middle	Trailer	DM 'D' End North Leading
3231	4231	4331	3331	3431	4531	3531
3232	4232	4332	3332	3432	4532	3532
3233	4233	4333	3333	3433	4533	3533
3234	4234	4334	3334	3434	4534	3534
3235	4235	4335	3335	3435	4535	3535
3236	4236	4336	3336	3436	4536	3536
3237	4237	4337	3337	3437	4537	3537
3238	4238	4338	3338	3438	4538	3538
3239	4239	4339	3339	3440	4540	3540
3240	4240	4340	3340	3441	4541	3541
3241	4241	4341	3341	3442	4542	3542
3242	4242	4342	3342	3443	4543	3543
3243	4243	4343	3343	3444	4544	3544
3244	4244	4344	3344	3445	4545	3545
3245	4245	4345	3345	3446	4546	3546
3246	4246	4346	3346	3447	4547	3547
3247	4247	4347	3347	3448	4548	3548
3248	4248	4348	3348	3449	4549	3549
3250	4250	4350	3350	3450	4550	3550
3251	4251	4351	3351	3451	4551	3551
3252	4252	4352(d)	3352	3452	4552	3552
3253	4253	4353(d)	3353	3453	4553	3553
3254	4254	4354(d)	3354	3454	4554	3554
3255	4255	4355(d)	3355	3455	4555	3555
3256	4256	4356(d)	3356	3456	4556	3556
3258	4258	4358(d)	3358	3457	4557	3557
3259	4259	4359(d)	3359	3458	4558	3558
3260	4260	4360(d)	3360	3459	4559	3559
3261	4261	4361(d)	3361	3460	4560	3560
3262	4262	4362(d)	3362	3461	4561	3561
3263	4263	4363(d)	3363	3462	4562	3562
3264*	4264*	4364*	3364*	3463	4563	3563
3265*	4265*	4365*	3365*	3464*	4564*	3564*
3266*	4266*	4366§	3366§	3465*	4565*	3565*
3267*	4267*	4367*	3367*	3466*	4566*	3566*
				3467*	4567*	3567*

(d) Fitted with de-icing equipment.
* 1972 MkI stock cars (renumbered).
§ Renumbered 1972 MkII stock cars.

1992 Tube Stock Two-car 'A' - 'B' Units

DM 'A' Car	NDM 'B' Car	DM 'A' Car	NDM 'B' Car	DM 'A' Car	NDM 'B' Car	DM 'A' Car	NDM 'B' Car
91001	92001	91089	92089	91177	92177	91265	92265
91003	92003	91091	92091	91179	92179	91267	92267
91005	92005	91093	92093	91181	92181	91269	92269
91007	92007	91095	92095	91183	92183	91271	92271
91009	92009	91097	92097	91185	92185	91273	92273
91011	92011	91099	92099	91187	92187	91275	92275
91013	92013	91101	92101	91189	92189	91277	92277
91015	92015	91103	92103	91191	92191	91279	92279
91017	92017	91105	92105	91193	92193	91281	92281
91019	92019	91107	92107	91195	92195	91283	92283
91021	92021	91109	92109	91197	92197	91285	92285
91023	92023	91111	92111	91199	92199	91287	92287
91025	92025	91113	92113	91201	92201	91289	92289
91027	92027	91115	92115	91203	92203	91291	92291
91029	92029	*91117*	*92117*	91205	92205	91293	92293
91031	92031	91119	92119	91207	92207	91295	92295
91033	92033	91121	92121	91209	92209	91297	92297
91035	92035	91123	92123	91211	92211	91299	92299
91037	92037	91125	92125	91213	92213	91301	92301
91039	92039	91127	92127	91215	92215	91303	92303
91041	92041	91129	92129	91217	92217	91305	92305
91043	92043	91131	92131	91219	92219	91307	92307
91045	*92045*	91133	92133	91221	92221	91309	92309
91047	92047	91135	92135	91223	92223	91311	92311
91049	92049	91137	92137	91225	92225	91313	92313
91051	92051	91139	92139	91227	92227	91315	92315
91053	92053	91141	92141	91229	92229	91317	92317
91055	92055	91143	92143	91231	92231	91319	92319
91057	92057	91145	92145	91233	92233	91321	92321
91059	92059	91147	92147	91235	92235	91323	92323
91061	92061	91149	92149	91237	92237	91325	92325
91063	92063	91151	92151	91239	92239	91327	92327
91065	92065	91153	92153	91241	92241	91329	92329
91067	92067	91155	92155	91243	92243	91331	92331
91069	92069	91157	92157	91245	92245	91333	92333
91071	92071	91159	92159	91247	92247	91335	92335
91073	92073	91161	92161	91249	92249	91337	92337
91075	92075	91163	92163	91251	92251	91339	92339
91077	92077	91165	92165	91253	92253	91341	92341
91079	92079	91167	92167	91255	92255	91343	92343
91081	92081	91169	92169	91257	92257	91345	92345
91083	92083	91171	92171	*91259*	*92259*	91347	92347
91085	92085	91173	92173	91261	92261	91349	92349
91087	92087	91175	92175	91263	92263		

1992 Tube Stock Two-car 'B' - 'D' De-icing Units

NDM 'B' Car	NDM 'D' Car	NDM 'B' Car	NDM 'D' Car	NDM 'B' Car	NDM 'D' Car	NDM 'B' Car	NDM 'D' Car
92402	93402	92418	93418	92434	93434	92450	93450
92404	93404	92420	93420	92436	93436	92452	93452
92406	93406	92422	93422	92438	93438	92454	93454
92408	93408	92424	93424	92440	93440	92456	93456
92410	93410	92426	93426	92442	93442	92458	93458
92412	93412	92428	93428	92444	93444	92460	93460
92414	93414	92430	93430	92446	93446	92462	93462
92416	93416	92432	93432	92448	93448	92464	93464

1992 Tube Stock Two-car 'B' - 'C' Units

NDM 'B' Car	NDM 'C' Car	NDM 'B' Car	NDM 'C' Car	NDM 'B' Car	NDM 'C' Car	NDM 'B' Car	NDM 'C' Car
92002	93002	92070	93070	92138	93138	92206	93206
92004	93004	92072	93072	92140	93140	92208	93208
92006	93006	92074	93074	92142	93142	92210	93210
92008	93008	92076	93076	92144	93144	92212	93212
92010	93010	92078	93078	92146	93146	92214	93214
92012	*93012*	92080	93080	92148	93148	92216	93216
92014	93014	92082	93082	92150	93150	92218	93218
92018	*93018*	92086	93086	92154	93154	92222	93222
92020	93020	92088	93088	92156	93156	92224	93224
92022	93022	92090	93090	92158	93158	92226	93226
92024	93024	92092	93092	92160	93160	92228	93228
92026	93026	92094	93094	92162	93162	92230	93230
92028	93028	92096	93096	92164	93164	92232	93232
92030	93030	92098	93098	92166	93166	92234	93234
92032	93032	92100	93100	92168	93168	92236	93236
92034	93034	92102	93102	92170	93170	92238	93238
92036	93036	92104	93104	92172	93172	92240	93240
92038	93038	92106	93106	92174	93174	92242	93242
92040	93040	92108	93108	92176	93176	92244	93244
92042	93042	92110	93110	92178	93178	92246	93246
92044	93044	92112	93112	92180	93180	92248	93248
92046	93046	92114	93114	92182	93182	92250	93250
92048	93048	92116	93116	92184	93184	92252	93252
92050	93050	92118	93118	92186	93186	92254	93254
92052	93052	92120	93120	92188	93188	92256	93256
92054	93054	92122	93122	92190	93190	92258	93258
92056	93056	92124	93124	92192	93192	92260	93260
92058	93058	92126	93126	92194	93194	92262	93262
92060	93060	92128	93128	92196	93196	92264	93264
92062	93062	92130	93130	92198	93198	92266	93266
92064	93064	92132	93132	92200	93200		
92066	93066	92134	93134	92202	93202		
92068	93068	92136	93136	92204	93204		

WATERLOO & CITY LINE

1992 Tube Stock Two-car 'E' - 'F' Units

DM 'E' Car	NDM 'F' Car	DM 'E' Car	NDM 'F' Car	DM 'E' Car	NDM 'F' Car	DM 'E' Car	NDM 'F' Car	DM 'E' Car	NDM 'F' Car
65501	67501	65503	67503	65505	67505	65507	67507	65509	67509
65502	67502	65504	67504	65506	67506	65508	67508	65510	67510

C69 & C77 Stock Two-car Units

DM	Uncoupling Trailer	DM	Uncoupling Trailer	DM	Uncoupling Trailer	DM	Uncoupling Trailer
5501	6501	5536	6536	5571	6571	5701	6701
5502	6502	5537	6537	5572	6572	5702	6702
5503	6503	5538	6538	5573	6573	5703	6703
5504	6504	5539	6539	5574	6574	5704	6704
5505	6505	5540	6540	5575	6575	5705	6705
5506	6506	5541	6541	5576	6576	5706	6706
5507	6507	5542	6542	5577	6577	5707	6707
5508	6508	5543	6543(d)	5578	6578	5708	6708
5509	6509	5544	6544(d)	5579	6579	5709	6709
5510	6510	5545	6545(d)	5580	6580	5710	6710
5511	6511	5546	6546(d)	5581	6581	5711	6711
5512	6512	5547	6547(d)	5582	6582	5712	6712
5513	6513	5548	6548(d)	5583	6583	5713	6713
5514	6514	5549	6549(d)	5584	6584	5714	6714
5515	6515	5550	6550(d)	5585	6585	5715	6715
5516	6516	5551	6551(d)	5586	6586	5716	6716
5517	6517	5552	6552(d)	5587	6587	5717	6717
5518	6518	5553	6553(d)	5588	6588	5718	6718
5519	6519	5554	6554*	5589	6589	5719	6719
5520	6520	*5555*	*6555**	5590	6590	5720	6720
5521	6521	5556	6556*	5591	6591	5721	6721
5522	6522	5557	6557	5592	6592	5722	6722
5523	6523	5558	6558	5593	6593	5723	6723
5524	6524	5559	6559	5594	6594	5724	6724
5525	6525	5560	6560	5595	6595	5725	6725
5526	6526	5561	6561	5596	6596	5726	6726
5527	6527	5562	6562	5597	6597	5727	6727
5528	*6528*	5563	6563	5598	6598	5728	6728
5529	6529	5564	6564	5599	6599	5729	6729
5530	6530	5565	6565	5600	6600	5730	6730
5531	6531	5566	6566	5601	6601	5731	6731
5532	6532	5567	6567§	5602	6602	5732	6732
5533	6533	5568	6568	5603	6603	5733	6733
5534	6534	5569	6569	5604	6604		
5535	6535	5570	6570	5605	6605		

(d) Fitted with de-icing equipment § Tinted glass car windows. * Former de-icing trailer.

DISTRICT LINE

D Stock Three-car Units
'A' Single-ended Units

'D' Single-ended Units

DM 'A' End West Leading	Trailer	UNDM 'D' End East Middle	UNDM 'A' End West Middle	Trailer	DM 'D' End East Leading
7000	17000(d)	8000	8001	17001	7001
7002	17002(d)	8002	8003	17003	7003
7004	17004(d)	8004	8005	17005	7005
7006	17006(d)	8006	8007	17007	7007
7008	17008(d)	8008	8009	17009	7009
7010	17010(d)	8010	8011	17011	7011
7012	17012(d)	8012	8013	17013	7013
7014	17014(d)	8014	8015	17015	7015
7016	17016(d)	8016	8017	17017	7017
7018	17018(d)	8018	8019	17019	7019
7020	17020(d)	8020	8021	17021	7021

D Stock Three-car Units continued

DM 'A' End West Leading	Trailer	UNDM 'D' End East Middle		UNDM 'A' End West Middle	Trailer	DM 'D' End East Leading
7022	17022(d)	8022		8023	17023	7023
7024	17024(d)	8024		8025	17025	7025
7026	17026(d)	8026		8027	17027	7027
7028	17028(d)	8028		8029	17029	7029
7030	17030(d)	8030		8031	17031	7031
7032	17032(d)	8032		8033	17033	7033
7034	17034(d)	8034		8035	17035*	7035
7036	17036(d)	8036		8037	17037	7037
7038	17038(d)	8038		8039	17039	7039
7040	17040(d)	8040		8041	17041	7041
7042	17042(d)	8042		† 8043	† 17043	† 7043
7044	17044(d)	8044		8045	17045	7045
7046	17046(d)	8046		8047	17047	7047
7048	17048(d)	8048		8049	17049	7049
7050	17050	8050		8051	17051	7051
7052	17052	8052		8053	17053	7053
7054	17054	8054		8055	17055	7055
7056	17056	8056		8057	17057	7057
7058	17058	8058		8059	17059	7059
7060	17060	8060		8061	17061	7061
7062	17062	8062		8063	17063	7063
7064	17064	8064		8065	17065	7065
7066	17066	8066		8067	17067	7067
7068	17068	8068		8069	17069	7069
7070	17070	8070		8071	17071	7071
7072	17072	8072		8073	17073	7073
7074	17074	8074		8075	17075	7075
7076	17076	8076		8077	17077*	7077
7078	17078	8078		8079	17079	7079
§7080	§17080	§8080		8081	17081	7081
7082	17082	8082		8083	17083	7083
7084	17084	8084		8085	17085	7085
7086	17086	8086		8087	17087	7087
7088	17088	8088		8089	17089	7089
7090	17090	8090		8091	17091	7091
7092	17092	8092		8093	17093	7093
7094	17094	8094		8095	17095	7095
7096	17096	8096		8097	17097	7097
7098	17098	8098		8099	17099	7099
7100	17100	8100		8101	17101	7101
7102	17102	8102		8103	17103	7103
7104	17104	8104		8105	17105	7105
7106	17106	8106		8107	17107	7107
7108	17108	8108		8109	17109	7109
7110	17110	8110		8111	17111	7111
7112	17112	8112		8113	17113	7113
7114	17114	8114		8115	17115	7115
7116	17116	8116		8117	17117	7117
7118	17118	8118		8119	17119	7119
7120	17120	8120		8121	17121	7121
7122	17122	8122		8123	17123	7123
7124	17124	8124		8125	17125	7125
7126	17126	8126		8127	17127	7127
7128	17128	8128		8129	17129	7129

D Stock Double-ended Units

DM 'A' End West	Trailer	DM 'D' End East	DM 'A' End West	Trailer	DM 'D' End East
7500	17500	7501	7520	17520	7521
7502	17502	7503	7522	17522	7523
7504	17504	7505	7524	17524	7525
7506	17506	7507	7526	17526	7527
7508	17508	7509	7528	17528	7529
7510	17510	7511	7530	17530	7531
7512	17512	7513	7532	17532	7533
7514	17514	7515	7534	17534	7535
7516	17516	7517	7536	17536	7537
7518	17518	7519	7538	17538	7539

* Trailers 17035 and 17077 were originally 17077 and 17035 respectively.
† Fitted with Knorr Bremse braking equipment.
§ Fitted with Westingouse analogue braking equipment.
(d) Fitted with de-icing equipment.

JUBILEE LINE

1983 Tube Stock Double-ended Three-car Units
Batch I   Batch II

DM 'A' End North	Trailer	DM 'D' End South	DM 'A' End North	Trailer	DM 'D' End South
3601	4601	3701	3631	4631(d)	3731
3602	4602	3702	3632	4632(d)	3732
3603	4603	3703	3633	4633(d)	3733
3604	4604	3704	3634	4634(d)	3734
3605	4605	3705	3635	4635(d)	3735
3606	4606	3706	3636	4636	3736
†3607	4607	†3707	3637	4637	3737
3608	4608	3708	3638	4638	3738
†3609	4609	†3709	3639	4639	3739
†3610	4610	†3710	3640	4640	3740
†3611	4611	†3711	3641	4641	3741
†3612	4612	†3712	3642	4642	3742
3613	4613	3713	3643	4643	3743
3614	4614	3714	3644	4644	3744
3615	4615	3715	3645	4645	3745
3616	4616	3716	3646	4646	3746
3617	4617	3717	3647	4647	3747
§3618	4618	3718	3648	4648	3748
3619	4619	3719	3649	4649	3749
3620	4620	3720	3650	4650	3750
3621	4621	3721	3651	4651	3751
3622	4622	3722	3652	4652	3752
3624	4624	3724	3653	4653	3753
3625	4625	3725	3654	4654	3754
3626	4626(d)	3726	3655	4655	3755
3627	4627(d)	3727	3656	4656	3756
3629	4629(d)	3729	3657	4657	3757
3630	4630(d)	3730*	3658	4658	3758
			3659	4659	3759
			3660	4660	3760
			3661	4661	3761
			3662	4662	3762
			3663	4663	3763

* DM 3730 was originally 3728.
† Cars retain original style front vents.
§ Car fitted with humidity sensors.
(d) Fitted with de-icing equipment.

1996 Tube Stock Three-car Units *being delivered 1996-1998*

DM 'A' End West Leading	Trailer	UNDM 'D' End Middle	UNDM 'A' End Middle	Trailer	DM 'D' End East Leading
96002	96202	96402	96401	96201	96001
96004	96204	96404	96403	96203	96003
96006	96206	96406	96405	96205	96005
96008	96208	96408	96407	96207	96007
96010	96210	96410	96409	96209	96009
96012	96212	96412	96411	96211	96011
96014	96214	96414	96413	96213	96013
96016	96216	96416	96415	96215	96015
96018	96218	96418	96417	96217	96017
96020	96220	96420	96419	96219	96019
96022	96222	96422	96421	96221	96021
96024	96224	96424	96423	96223	96023
96026	96226	96426	96425	96225	96025
96028	96228	96428	96427	96227	96027
96030	96230	96430	96429	96229	96029
96032	96232	96432	96431	96231	96031
96034	96234	96434	96433	96233	96033
96036	96236	96436	96435	96235	96035
96038	96238	96438	96437	96237	96037
96040	96240	96440	96439	96239	96039
96042	96242	96442	96441	96241	96041
96044	96244	96444	96443	96243	96043
96046	96246	96446	96445	96245	96045
96048	96248	96448	96447	96247	96047
96050	96250	96450	96449	96249	96049
96052	96252	96452	96451	96251	96051
96054	96254	96454	96453	96253	96053
96056	96256	96456	96455	96255	96055
96058	96258	96458	96457	96257	96057
96060	96260	96460	96459	96259	96059
96062	96262	96462	96461	96261	96061
96064	96264	96464	96463	96263	96063
96066	96266	96466	96465	96265	96065
96068	96268	96468	96467	96267	96067
96070	96270	96470	96469	96269	96069
96072	96272	96472	96471	96271	96071
96074	96274	96474	96473	96273	96073
96076	96276	96476	96475	96275	96075
96078	96278	96478	96477	96277	96077
96080	96880(d)	96480	96479	96279	96079
96082	96882(d)	96482	96481	96281	96081
96084	96884(d)	96484	96483	96283	96083
96086	96886(d)	96486	96485	96285	96085
96088	96888(d)	96488	96487	96287	96087
96090	96890(d)	96490	96489	96289	96089
96092	96892(d)	96492	96491	96291	96091
96094	96894(d)	96494	96493	96293	96093
96096	96896(d)	96496	96495	96295	96095
96098	96898(d)	96498	96497	96297	96097
96100	96900(d)	96500	96499	96299	96099
96102	96902(d)	96502	96501	96301	96101
96104	96904(d)	96504	96503	96303	96103
96106	96906(d)	96506	96505	96305	96105
96108	96908(d)	96508	96507	96307	96107
96110	96910(d)	96510	96509	96309	96109
96112	96912(d)	96512	96511	96311	96111
96114	96914(d)	96514	96513	96313	96113
96116	96916(d)	96516	96515	96315	96115
96118	96918(d)	96518	96517	96317	96117

(d) Fitted with de-icing equipment.

A60/62 Stock Four-car Units

DM 'A' End North	Trailer	Trailer	DM 'D' End South	DM 'A'End North	Trailer	Trailer	DM 'D' End South
5056	6056	6057	5057	5102	6102(d)	6103	5103
5058	6058	6059	5059	5104	6104(d)	6105	5105
5060	6060	6061	5061	5106	6106(d)	6107	5107
5062	6062	6063	5063	5108	6108(d)	6109	5109
5064	6064	6065	5065	5110	6110(d)	6111	5111
5066	6066	6067	5067	5112	6112(d)	6113	5113
5088	6088(d)	6089	5089	5114	6114(d)	6115	5115
5090	6090(d)	6091	5091	5116*	6116(d)	6117*	5117*
5092	6092(d)	6093	5093	5118	6118(d)	6119	5119
5094	6094(d)	6095	5095	5120	6120(d)	6121	5121*
5096	§6096(d)	6097	5097	5122	6122(d)	6123	5123
5098	6098(d)	6099	5099	5232*	6232*	6233*	5233*
5100	6100(d)	6101	5101	5234*	6234(d)*	6235*	5235*

DM 'A' End North Leading	Trailer	Trailer	DM 'D' End South Middle	DM 'A' End North Middle	Trailer	Trailer	DM 'D' End South Leading
5000	6000(d)	6001	5001	5140	6140	6141	5141
5002	6002	6003	5003	5144	6144	6145	5145
5004	6004(d)	6005	5005	5146	6146	6147	5147
5006	6006	6007	5007	5148	6148	6149	5149
5010	6010	6011	5011	5150	6150	6151	5151
5012	6012	6013	5013	5152	6152	6153	5153
5014	6014	6015	5015	5154	6154	6155	5155
5016	6016	6017	5017	5156	6156	6157	5157
5018	6018	6019	5019	5158	6158	6159	5159
5020	6020	6021	5021	5160	6160	6161	5161
5022	6022	6023	5023	5162	6162	6163	5163
5024	6024	6025	5025	5164	6164	6165	5165
5026	6026	6027	5027	5166	6166	6167	5167
5030	6030	6031	5031	5168	6168	6169	5169
5032	6032	6033	5033	5172	6172	6173	5173
5034*	6034	6035	5035	5174	6174	6175	5175
5038	6038	6039	5039	5176	6176	6177	5177
5040	6040	6041	5041	5178	6178	6179	5179
5042	6042	6043	5043	5180	6180	6181	5181
5044	6044	6045	5045	5182	6182	6183	5183
5046	6046	6047	5047	5184	6184	6185	5185
5048	6048	6049	5049	5186	6186	6187	5187
5050	6050	6051	5051	5188	6188	6189	5189
5052	6052	6053	5053	5190	6190	6191	5191
5054	6054	6055	5055	5192	6192	6193	5193
5068	6068	6069	5069	5194	6194	6195	5195
5070	6070	6071	5071	5196	6196	6197	5197
5072	6072	6073	5073	5198	6198	6199	5199
5074	6074	6075	5075	5200	6200	6201	5201
5076	6076	6077	5077	5202	6202	6203	5203
5078	6078	6079	5079	5204	6204	6205	5205
5080	6080	6081	5081	5206	6206	6207	5207
5082	6082	6083	5083	5210	6210	6211	5211
5084	6084	6085	5085	5212	6212	6213	5213
5086	6086	6087	5087	5214	6214	6215	5215
5124	6124	6125	5125	5216	6216	6217	5217
5126	6126	6127	5127	5218*	6218	6219	5219
5128	6128	6129	5129	5220	6220	6221	5221
5130	6130	6131	5131	5222	6222	6223	5223
5132	6132	6133	5133	5224	6224	6225	5225
5134	6134	6135	5135	5226	6226	6227	5227
5136	6136	6137	5137	5228	6228	6229	5229
5138	6138	6139	5139	5230	6230	6231	5231
5142	6142	6143	5143				

(d) Fitted with de-icing equipment.   * Cars renumbered.   § Tinted glass car windows.

1959 Tube Stock

DM 'A' End North Leading	Trailer	NDM	DM 'D' End South Middle	DM 'A' End North Middle	Trailer	DM 'D' End South Leading
1012	2012	9013	1013	1014	2014	1015
1016	2016	9017	1017	1018	2018	1019
1020	2020	9021	1021	1022	2022	1023
1024	2024	9025	1025	1026	2026	1027
1028	2028	9029	1029(r)	1030	2030	1031*(p)
1032	2032	9033	1033	1034	2034	1035
1036	2036(h)	9037	1037	1038	2038	1039
1040	2040	9041	1041	1042	2042	1043(r)
1044	2044	9045	1045(p)	1046	2046	1047
1048	2048	9049	1049	1050	2050	1051
1056	2056	9057	1057	1054	2054(h)	1055
1060	2060	9061	1061	1058	2058	1059
1064	2064	9065	1065	1062	2062	1063
1068	2068	9069	1069	1066	2066	1067
1072	2072	9073	1073	1074	2074	1075
1076	2076	9077	1077	1078	2078	1079
1080	2080	9081	1081	1082	2082	1083
1084	2084	9085	1053	1090	2090	1091
1088	2088	9089	1089	1094	2094	1095
1092	2092	9093	1093	1098	2098	1099
1096	2096	9097	1097	1102	2102	1103
1100	2100(d)	9101	1101	1106	2106	1107
1104	2104(d)	9105	1105	1110	2110(h)	1111
1108	2108(d)	9109	1109	1114	2114	1115
1112	2112(d)	9113	1113	1118	2118	1119
1116	2116(d)	9117	1117	1126	2126	1127
1120	2120(d)	9121	1121	1130	2130	1131
1124	2124(d)	9125	1125	1134	2134	1135
1128	2128(d)	9129	1129	1138	2138	1139
1132	2132(d)	9133	1133	1142	2142	1143
1136	2136(d)	9137	1137	1146	2146	1147
1140	2140(d)	9141	1141	1150	2150	1151
1144	2144(d)	9145	1145	1154	2154	1155
1148	2148(d)	9149	1149	1158	2158	1159
1152	2152(d)	9153	1153	1162	2162	1163
1156	2156(d)	9157	1157	1166	2166	1167
1160	2160(d)	9161	1161	1170	2170	1171
1164	2164(d)	9165	1165	1174	2174	1175
1168	2168(d)	9169	1169	1178	2178	1179
1172	2172(d)	9173	1173	1182	2182	1183
1176	2176(d)	9177	1177	1186	2186	1187
1180	2180(d)	9181	1181	1194	2194	1195
1184	2184(d)	9185	1185	1198	2198	1199
1188	2188(d)	9189	1189	1202	2202	1203
1192	2192(d)	9193	1193	1210	2210	1211
1196	2196(d)	9197	1197	1214	2214	1215
1200	2200(d)	9201	1201	1218	2218	1219
1204	2204(d)	9205	1205	1222	2222	1223
1208	2208(d)	9209	1209	1226	2226	1227
1212	2212(d)	9213	1213	1230	2230	1231
1216	2216(d)	9217	1217	1234	2234	1235
1220	2220	9221	1221	1238	2238	1239
1224	2224	9225	1225	1242	2242	1243
1228	2228	9229	1229	1246	2246	1247
1232	2232	9233	1233	1250	2250	1251
1236	2236	9237	1237	1254	2254	1255
1240	2240	9241	1241	1258	2258	1259
1244	2244	9245	1245	1262	2262	1263
1248	2248	9249	1249	1266	2266	1267
1252	2252	9253	1253	1270	2270	1271
1256	2256	9257	1257	1274	2274	1275

1959 Tube Stock continued

DM 'A' End North Leading	Trailer	NDM	DM 'D' End South Middle	DM 'A' End North Middle	Trailer	DM 'D' End South Leading
1264	2264	9265	1265	1278	2278	1279
1268	2268	9269	1269	1282	2282	1283
1272	2272	9273	1273	1290	2290	1291
1276	2276	9277	1277	1294	2294	1295
1280	2280	9281	1281	1298	2298	1299
1284	2284	9285	1285	1302	2302	1303
1288	2288	9289	1289	1306	2306	1307
1292	2292	9293	1293	1310	2310	1311
1296	2296	9297	1297	1314	2314	1315
1300	2300	9301	1301			
1304	2304	9305	1305			
1308	2308	9309	1309R*			
1312	2312	9313	1313			

1962 Tube Stock

DM 'A' End North Leading	Trailer	NDM	DM 'D' End South Middle	DM 'A' End North Middle	Trailer	DM 'D' End South Leading
1404	2404	9405	1405	1574	2574	1575
1428	2428	9429	1429	1604	2604	1605
1464	2464	9465	1465	1678	2678*	1679
1514	2514	§9515	1515	1682	2682*	1683
1522	2522*	§9525	1523	1740	2740	1741
1738	2738	9739	1739	1746	2746	1747
1744	2744	9745	1745	1748	2748	1749
				1750	2750	1751

1972 MkI Tube Stock

DM 'A' End North Leading	Trailer	Trailer	DM 'D' End South Middle	UNDM 'A' End North Middle	Trailer	DM 'D' End South Leading
3201	4201	4301	3301	3402	4502	3502
3202	4202	4302	3302(a)	3404	4504	3504
3205	4205(f)	4330	3305	3407	4507	3507
3206	4206	4306	3306	3408	4508	3508
3207	4207	4307	3307	3409	4509	3509
3208	4208	4308	3308	3410	4510	3510
3209	4209	4309	3309	3411	4511	3511
3211	4211	4311	3311	3413	4513	3513
3212	4212	4312	3312	3414	4514	3514
3213	4213	4313	3313	3415	4515	3515
3214	4214	4314	3314	3417	4517(f)	3517
3215	4215	4315	3315	3418	4518	3518(a)
3219	4219	4319	3319	3419	4519	3519
3221	4221	4321	3321	3421	4521	3521
3222	4222	4322	3322	3422	4522	3522(a)
3226	4226	4326	3326	3423	4523	3523(a)
3227	4227	4327	3327(a)	3425	4525	3525
3228	4228	4328	3328	3426	4503	3503
3229	4229	4329	3329	3428	4528	3528
3230	4230	4305	3330	3430	4530	3530

* Cars renumbered.
§ 1959 stock NDM.
(a) Painted units - see text for details.
(d) Fitted with de-icing equipment.
(f) Experimental tiled flooring surfaces.
(h) Fitted with thermostatically-controlled car heaters.
(p) Painted in 1920s 'Heritage' livery.
(r) Refurbished units, painted in Corporate 'red doors' livery.

1995 Tube Stock Three-car Units

BEING DELIVERED 1996-1998

DM 'D' End Leading	Trailer	UNDM 'A' End Middle	UNDM 'D' End Middle	Trailer	DM 'A' End Leading
51501	52501	53501	53502	52502	51502
51503	52503	53503	53504	52504	51504
51505	52505	53505	53506	52506	51506
51507	52507	53507	53508	52508	51508
51509	52509	53509	53510	52510	51510
51511	52511	53511	53512	52512	51512
51513	52513	53513	53514	52514	51514
51515	52515	53515	53516	52516	51516
51517	52517	53517	53518	52518	51518
51519	52519	53519	53520	52520	51520
51521	52521	53521	53522	52522	51522
51523	52523	53523	53524	52524	51524
51525	52525	53525	53526	52526	51526
51527	52527	53527	53528	52528	51528
51529	52529	53529	53530	52530	51530
51531	52531	53531	53532	52532	51532
51533	52533	53533	53534	52534	51534
51535	52535	53535	53536	52536	51536
51537	52537	53537	53538	52538	51538
51539	52539	53539	53540	52540	51540
51541	52541	53541	53542	52542	51542
51543	52543	53543	53544	52544	51544
51545	52545	53545	53546	52546	51546
51547	52547	53547	53548	52548	51548
51549	52549	53549	53550	52550	51550
51551	52551	53551	53552	52552	51552
51553	52553	53553	53554	52554	51554
51555	52555	53555	53556	52556	51556
51557	52557	53557	53558	52558	51558
51559	52559	53559	53560	52560	51560
51561	52561	53561	53562	52562	51562
51563	52563	53563	53564	52564	51564
51565	52565	53565	53566	52566	51566
51567	52567	53567	53568	52568	51568
51569	52569	53569	53570	52570	51570
51571	52571	53571	53572	52572	51572
51573	52573	53573	53574	52574	51574
51575	52575	53575	53576	52576	51576
51577	52577	53577	53578	52578	51578
51579	52579	53579	53580	52580	51580
51581	52581	53581	53582	52582	51582
51583	52583	53583	53584	52584	51584
51585	52585	53585	53586	52586	51586
51587	52587	53587	53588	52588	51588
51589	52589	53589	53590	52590	51590
51591	52591	53591	53592	52592	51592
51593	52593	53593	53594	52594	51594
51595	52595	53595	53596	52596	51596
51597	52597	53597	53598	52598	51598
51599	52599	53599	53600	52600	51600
51601	52601	53601	53602	52602	51602
51603	52603	53603	53604	52604	51604
51605	52605	53605	53606	52606	51606
51607	52607	53607	53608	52608	51608
51609	52609	53609	53610	52610	51610
51611	52611	53611	53612	52612	51612
51613	52613	53613	53614	52614	51614
51615	52615	53615	53616	52616	51616
51617	52617	53617	53618	52618	51618
51619	52619	53619	53620	52620	51620
51621	52621	53621	53622	52622	51622
51623	52623	53623	53624	52624	51624

DM 'D' End Leading	Trailer	UNDM 'A' End Middle	UNDM 'D' End Middle	Trailer	DM 'A' End Leading
51625	52625	53625	53626	52626	51626
51627	52627	53627	53628	52628	51628
51629	52629	53629	53630	52630	51630
51631	52631	53631	53632	52632	51632
51633	52633	53633	53634	52634	51634
51635	52635	53635	53636	52636	51636
51637	52637	53637	53638	52638	51638
51639	52639	53639	53640	52640	51640
51641	52641	53641	53642	52642	51642
51643	52643	53643	53644	52644	51644
51645	52645	53645	53646	52646	51646
51647	52647	53647	53648	52648	51648
51649	52649	53649	53650	52650	51650
51651	52651	53651	53652	52652	51652
51653	52653	53653	53654	52654	51654
51655	52655	53655	53656	52656	51656
51657	52657	53657	53658	52658	51658
51659	52659	53659	53660	52660	51660
51661	52661	53661	53662	52662	51662
51663	52663	53663	53664	52664	51664
51665	52665	53665	53666	52666	51666
51667	52667	53667	53668	52668	51668
51669	52669	53669	53670	52670	51670
51671	52671	53671	53672	52672	51672
51673	52673	53673	53674	52674	51674
51675	52675	53675	53676	52676	51676
51677	52677	53677	53678	52678	51678
51679	52679	53679	53680	52680	51680
51681	52681	53681	53682	52682	51682
51683	52683	53683	53684	52684	51684
51685	52685	53685	53686	52686	51686

1995 Tube Stock
Three-car 'D' End De-icing Units   Three-car 'A' End De-icing Units

DM 'D' End Leading	De-icing Trailer	UNDM 'A' End Middle	UNDM 'D' End Middle	De-icing Trailer	DM 'A' End Leading
51701	52701	53701	53702	52702	51702
51703	52703	53703	53704	52704	51704
51705	52705	53705	53706	52706	51706
51707	52707	53707	53708	52708	51708
51709	52709	53709	53710	52710	51710
51711	52711	53711	53712	52712	51712
51713	52713	53713	53714	52714	51714
51715	52715	53715	53716	52716	51716
51717	52717	53717	53718	52718	51718
51719	52719	53719	53720	52720	51720
51721	52721	53721	53722	52722	51722
51723	52723	53723	53724	52724	51724
51725	52725	53725	53726	52726	51726

1973 Tube Stock

DM 'A' End West Leading	Trailer	UNDM 'D' End East Middle	UNDM 'A' End West Middle	Trailer	DM 'D' End East Leading
100	500	300	301	501	101
102	502	302	303	503	103
104	504	304	305	505	105
106	506	306	307	507	107
108	508	308	309	509	109
110	510	310	311	511	111
112	512	312	313	513	113
116	516	316	315	515	115
118	518	318	317	517	117
120	520	320	319	519	119
122	522	322	321	521	121
124	524	324	323	523	123
126	526	326	325	525	125
128	528	328	327	527	127
130	530	330	329	529	129
132	532	332	331	531	131
134	534	334	333	533	133
136	536	336	335	535	135
138	538	338	337	537	137
140	540	340	339	539	139
142	542	342	341	541	141
144	544	344	343	543	143
146	546	346	345	545	145
148	548	348	347	547	147
150	550	350	349	549	149
152	552	352	351	551	151
154	554	354	353	553	153
156	556	356	355	555	155
158	558	358	357	557	157
160	560	360	359	559	159
162	562	362	361	561	161
164	564	364	363	563	163
166	566	366	365	565	165
168	568	368	367	567	167(p)
170	570	370	369	569	169
172	572	372	371	571	171
174	574	374	373	573	173
176	576	376	375	575	175
178	578	378	377	577	177
180	580	380	379	579	179
182	582	382	381	581	181
184	584	384	383	583	183
186	586	386	385	585	185
188	588	388	387	587	187
190	590	390	389	589	189
192	592	392	391	591	191
194	594	394	393	593	193
196	596	396(p)	395	595	195
198	598	398	397	597	197
200	600	400	399	599	199
202	602	402	401	601	201
206	606(d)	406	403	603	203
208	608(d)	408	405	605	205
210	610(d)	410	407	607	207
212	612(d)	412	409	609	209
214	614(d)	414	411	611	211
216	616(d)	416	413	613	213

(d) Fitted with de-icing equipment.
(p) Painted in all-over advertisement livery for United Airlines.

1973 Tube Stock continued

DM 'A' End West Leading	Trailer	UNDM 'D' End East Middle	UNDM 'A' End West Middle	Trailer	DM 'D' End East Leading
218	618(d)	418	415	615	215
220	620(d)	420	417	617	217
222	622(d)	422	419	619	219
224	624(d)	424	421	621	221
226	626(d)	426	423	623	223
228	628(d)	428	425	625	225
230	630(d)	430	427	627	227
232	632(d)	432	429	629	229
234	634(d)	434	431	631	231
236	636(d)	436	433	633	233
238	638(d)	438	435	635	235
240	640(d)	440	437	637	237
242	642(d)	442	439	639	239
244	644(d)	444	441	641	241
246	646(d)	446	443	643	243
248	648(d)	448	445	645	245
250	650(d)	450	447	647	247
252	652(d)	452	449	649	249
			451	651	251
			453	653	253

1973 Tube Stock Double-ended Units

DM 'A' End West	Trailer	DM 'D' End East	DM 'A' End West	Trailer	DM 'D' End East
854	654	855	876	676	877
856	656	857	878	678	879
858	658	859	880	680	881
860	660	861	882	682	883
862	662	863	884	684	885
864	664	865	886	686	887
866	666	867	890	690	891
868	668	869	†892	692	893
870	670	871	§894	694	895
872	672	873	896*	696*	897*
874	674	875			

* Cars renumbered.
† Formerly Westinghouse ETT.
§ Unit formerly GEC ETT, now fitted with Davies & Metcalfe braking.
(d) Fitted with de-icing equipment.

1967/72 Tube Stock

'A' End Units   'D' End Units

DM 'A' End North Leading	Trailer	Trailer	DM 'D' End South Middle	DM 'A' End North Middle	Trailer	Trailer	DM 'D' End South Leading
3001	4001	4101*	3101*	3002	4002	4102	3102
3003	4003	4103*	3103*	3004	4004	4104	3104
3005	4005	4105*	3105*	3006	4006	4106	3106
3007	4007	4107*	3107*	3008	4008	4108	3108
3009	4009	4109	3109	3010	4010	4110	3110
3011	4011	4111	3111	3013	4013	4113	3113
3012	4012	4112	3112	3014	4014	4114	3114
3016*	4016*	4116†	3116*	3015	4015	4115	3115
3017	4017	4117	3117	3019	4019	4119	3119
3018	4018	4118	3118	3021	4021	4121	3121
3020	4020	4120	3120	3023	4023	4123	3123
3022	4022	4122*	3122*	3025	4025	4125	3125
3024	4024	4124	3124	3027	4027	4127	3127
3026	4026	4126	3126	3031	4031	4131	3131
3028	4028	4128	3128	3032	4032	4132	3132
3029	4029	4129	3129	3033	4033	4133	3133
3030	4030	4130	3130	3038	4038	4138	3138
3034	4034	4134	3134	3039	4039	4139	3139
3035	4035	4135	3135	3040	4040	4140	3140
3036	4036	4136	3136	3044	4044	4144	3144
3037	4037	4137	3137	3049	4049	4149	3149
3041	4041	4141*	3141*	3051	4051	4151	3151
3042	4042	4142	3142	3053	4053	4153	3153
3043	4043	4143	3143	3055	4055	4155	3155
3045	4045	4145	3145	3057	4057	4157	3157
3046	4046	4146	3146	3080*†	4080*†	4180*	3180*
3047	4047	4147	3147	3081*†	4081*†	4181*	3181*
3048	4048	4148	3148	3082*†	4082*†	4182*	3182*
3050	4050	4150	3150	3083*†	4083*†	4183*	3183*
3052	4052	4152*	3152*	3084*†	4084*†	4184*	3184*
3054	4054	4154	3154	3085*†	4085*†	4185*	3185*
3056	4056	4156	3156	3086*†	4086*†	4186*	3186*

* Cars renumbered.
† 1972 MkI stock cars converted and renumbered to operate with 1967 stock.

1967/72 Tube Stock Double-ended Units

DM 'A' End North	Trailer	Trailer	DM 'D' End South	DM 'A' End North	Trailer	Trailer	DM 'D' End South
3058	4058	4158	3158	3069	4069	4169	3169
3059	4059	4159	3159	3070	4070	4170	3170
3060	4060	4160	3160	3071	4071	4171	3171
3061	4061	4161	3161	3072	4072	4172	3172
3062	4062	4162	3162	3073	4073	4173	3173
3063	4063	4163	3163	3074	4074	4174	3174
3064	4064	4164	3164	3075	4075	4175	3175
3065	4065	4165	3165	3076	4076	4176	3176
3066	4066	4166	3166	3077	4077	4177	3177
3067	4067	4167	3167	3078	4078	4178	3178
3068	4068	4168	3168	3079	4079	4179	3179

STOCK OUT OF SERVICE

Ex-Central Line 1962 Tube Stock

DM 'A' End	Trailer	NDM	NDM	DM 'D' End	
1406	2406(d)	9407	9601	1407	Track inspection (ATP fitted)
1440	9440	9441	–	1441	Pilot unit spare
–	–	–	9459	–	Sandite Car
1532	–	9533	–	–	Acton Works for ERU training
1560	2560	9561	–	1561	Northern & JLE pilot
1570	2570*	9571	–	1571	Acton Works
1576	2576(d)	9577	–	1577	Northfields depot
1630	2630	9631	–	1631	Northern & JLE pilot
1680	2680	–	–	1681	Northern Line track inspection
1690	2690	9691	–	1691	Northfields – Piccadilly Line

Ex-Central Line 1960 Tube Stock

DM 'A' End West Leading	Trailer (1938 Conv'n)	DM 'D' End East Leading	
3908	4921(d)	3909	For scrap – Hainault

Miscellaneous Cars

DM	Trailer	UNDM	
3016†	–	–	1967 Tube Stock - Northumberland Park depot for scrap
–	–	3439	1972 MkII Tube Stock - Acton Works - spare
3357	4257	–	1972 MkII Tube Stock - Stonebridge Park depot - spare
–	4357	–	1972 MkII Tube Stock - Stonebridge Park depot - spare
–	–	314	1973 Tube Stock - at Bombardier, Wakefield
204	604(d)	404	1973 Tube Stock - at Bombardier, Wakefield, withdrawn
3628	4628	–	1983 (batch I) Tube Stock - Northfields depot
3728†	–	–	1983 (batch I) Tube Stock - Northfields depot
–	6036	–	A60 Stock 'Sandite' car - Neasden depot

(d) Fitted with de-icing equipment.
† Original unrefurbished DM 3016. A refurbished 3016 is in service on the Victoria Line. DM 3728 was originally 3730.
* Renumbered 1962 stock trailers.

ENGINEERS' VEHICLE LIST

Battery Locomotives 37

No.	Deliv.	Builder	No.	Deliv.	Builder
‡L15	1970	Metro-Cammell	‡L45	1974	Metro-Cammell
‡L16	1970	Metro-Cammell	†‡L46	1974	Metro-Cammell
‡L17	1971	Metro-Cammell	†‡L47	1974	Metro-Cammell
‡L18	1971	Metro-Cammell	‡L48	1974	Metro-Cammell
‡L19	1971	Metro-Cammell	†‡L49	1974	Metro-Cammell
‡L20	1964	Metro-Cammell	†‡L50	1974	Metro-Cammell
‡L21	1964	Metro-Cammell	‡L51	1974	Metro-Cammell
L22	1965	Metro-Cammell	†‡L52	1974	Metro-Cammell
L23	1965	Metro-Cammell	†‡L53	1974	Metro-Cammell
L24	1965	Metro-Cammell	‡L54	1974	Metro-Cammell
L25	1965	Metro-Cammell	*L58	1952	Pickering
L26	1965	Metro-Cammell	*L59	1952	Pickering
L27	1965	Metro-Cammell	*L62	1985	Metro-Cammell
L28	1965	Metro-Cammell	*L63	1985	Metro-Cammell
L29	1965	Metro-Cammell	*L64	1985	Metro-Cammell
L30	1965	Metro-Cammell	*L65	1985	Metro-Cammell
L31	1965	Metro-Cammell	*L66	1986	Metro-Cammell
L32	1965	Metro-Cammell	*L67	1986	Metro-Cammell
†‡L44	1974	Metro-Cammell			

* Withdrawn from service.   †Painted blue.   ‡Fitted with ATP equipment.

Tube Stock Pilot and Ballast Motor Cars 4

No.	Origin	Converted	Previous No.	Built by	Type
†L132	1960	1987 BREL	3901	Cravens	Pilot
†L133	1960	1987 BREL	3905	Cravens	Pilot
L150	1938	1978 Acton	*10327	Metro-Cammell	Weed Killer
L151	1938	1978 Acton	*11327	Metro-Cammell	Weed Killer

* These cars were originally numbered 90327 and 91327 respectively.
† Fitted with buckeye couplers at inner ends at 'main line' height.

Bogie Flat Wagons (30 tons capacity) 7

F340	F344	F351	F355	F357	F366	F398

Builders: F340 Gloucester 1937, F344–366 Gloucester 1951, F398 BR Ashford 1965

Bogie Hopper Wagons (30 tons capacity) 22

HW201	HW204	HW207	HW210	HW213	HW216	HW219	HW222
HW202	HW205	HW208	HW211	HW214	HW217	HW220	
HW203	HW206	HW209	HW212	HW215	HW218	HW221	

Rail Wagons (20 tons capacity) 15

†RW490	†RW492	†RW494	*RW496	*RW498	*RW501	*RW503	RW506
†RW491	†RW493	RW495	*RW497	RW499	*RW502	RW505	

* Withdrawn from service.
† Formed into five-car set for long-rail-train operation.

Diesel Cranes 6

No.	Builder	Year	No.	Builder	Year
C623	Cowan Sheldon	1982	DHC627	Cowan Sheldon	1986
C624	Cowan Sheldon	1984	DHC628	Cowan Boyd	1993
C625	Cowan Sheldon	1984			
C626	Cowan Sheldon	1984			

Track Recording Car 1

TRC666   Converted 1987, ex-1973 stock trailer 514. Fitted with buckeye couplers at 'main line' height.

Plasser-Theurer Track Maintenance Machines 3

No.	Date New	Type	
*TMM771	1980	PU0716 Tamping Machine	
TMM772	1980	PU0716 Tamping Machine	Yellow livery
TMM773	1980	PU0716 Tamping Machine	

* Fitted with ATP equipment for use on the Central Line.

Unimog Road/Rail Vehicles 3

No.	Type	Date	Reg. No.	Use
*TMM774	Motor	1982	A723LNW	Leaf Clearing
*TMM775	Trailer			
L84	Motor	1983	A456NWX	Depot Shunter
L85	Motor	1986	C622EWT	Depot Shunter

* Withdrawn from service.
All are in yellow livery.

Rail Wagons (20 tonnes capacity) 26
Built 1986 by Procor, fitted with buckeye couplers

RW801	RW805	RW809	RW812	RW815	RW818	RW821	RW824
RW802	RW806	RW810	RW813	RW816	RW819	RW822	RW825
RW803	RW807	RW811	RW814	RW817	RW820	RW823	RW826
RW804	RW808						

High-Deck Wagons (40 tonnes capacity) 6
Built 1987 by Procor, fitted with buckeye couplers

HD871	HD872	HD873	HD874	HD875	HD876

General Purpose Wagons (30 tonnes capacity) 41

GP901	GP907	GP912	GP917	GP922	GP927	GP932	GP937
GP902	GP908	GP913	GP918	GP923	GP928	GP933	GP938
GP903	GP909	GP914	GP919	GP924	GP929	GP934	GP939
GP904	GP910	GP915	GP920	GP925	GP930	GP935	GP940
GP905	GP911	GP916	GP921	GP926	GP931	GP936	GP941
GP906							

Cement Mixer/Match Wagons 12
Built 1987 by Procor, fitted with buckeye couplers, yellow livery
Operated as CM/MW coupled twin units

CM950	CM952	CM954	MW956	MW958	MW960
CM951	CM953	CM955	MW957	MW959	MW961

Cable Drum Wagons 6

CW1050	CW1051	CW1052	Built 1940 by Gloucester (yellow livery 1984)
CW1053	CW1054	CW1055	Built 1996 by Bombardier (yellow livery)

Tunnel Cleaning Train 1

TCC1	Driving Motor 'A' end ex–1938 stock DM 10226
TCC2	Filter Car
TCC3	Nozzle Car } Built 1972–77 Acton Works
TCC4	Filter Car
TCC5	Driving Motor 'D' end ex–1938 stock DM 10087

Yellow Livery

Jubilee Line Extension Diesel Locomotives 14
Built 1996 by Schoma, Germany, yellow livery

No.	Name	No.	Name
1	Britta Lotta	8	Emma
2	Nikki	9	Debora
3	Claire	10	Clementine
4	Pam	11	Joan
5	Sophie	12	Melanie
6	Denise	13	Michele
7	Annemarie	14	Carol

Jubilee Line Extension General Purpose Wagons 15
Built 1994 by Bombardier

JLE1	JLE3	JLE5	JLE7	JLE9	JLE11	JLE13	JLE15
JLE2	JLE4	JLE6	JLE8	JLE10	JLE12	JLE14	

Jubilee Line Extension Bogie Well Wagons 4
Built 1994 by Bombardier

JLE16	JLE17	JLE18	JLE19

Jubilee Line Extension 4-wheel Cable Drum Wagons 4
Built 1994 by Bombardier

JLE20	JLE21	JLE22	JLE23

Turbot Wagons (34 tonnes capacity) 60
Built 1982–1988 variously by BR Shildon and Swindon, and RFS Doncaster. Converted by ABB Crewe in 1995. SB231–239 have 'long' drawgear, SB 240–290 'short' drawgear. Yellow livery.

No.	Former DB No.	No.	Former DB No.	No.	Former DB No.
SB231	978865	SB251	978753	SB271	978617
SB232	978047	SB252	978884	SB272	978699
SB233	978916	SB253	978767	SB273	978678
SB234	978864	SB254	978143	SB274	978682
SB235	978820	SB255	978886	SB275	978685
SB236	978702	SB256	978653	SB276	978688
SB237	978677	SB257	978626	SB277	978773
SB238	978788	SB258	978016	SB278	978783
SB239	978809	SB259	978026	SB279	978787
SB240	978647	SB260	978028	SB280	978797
SB241	978652	SB261	978051	SB281	978808
SB242	978766	SB262	978076	SB282	978810
SB243	978897	SB263	978086	SB283	978824
SB244	978898	SB264	978145	SB284	978830
SB245	978088	SB265	978161	SB285	978846
SB246	978901	SB266	978211	SB286	978858
SB247	978628	SB267	978318	SB287	978869
SB248	978003	SB268	978408	SB288	978892
SB249	978614	SB269	978420	SB289	978895
SB250	978700	SB270	978608	SB290	978918

CAR LAYOUTS

These are diagrammatic drawings only. All stock, with the exception of 1983 DM ends, has slightly chamfered ends. Doors are officially identified by letters as shown.

1959/62 Tube Stock

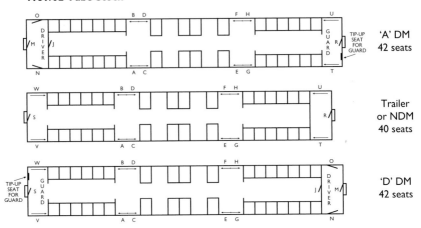

'A' DM
42 seats

Trailer
or NDM
40 seats

'D' DM
42 seats

1967/72 Tube Stock

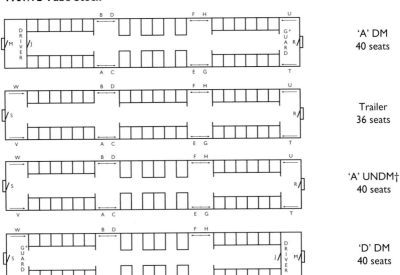

'A' DM
40 seats

Trailer
36 seats

'A' UNDM†
40 seats

'D' DM
40 seats

* On 1972 MkI trains on Northern Line only
† 1972 Stock only

1973 Tube Stock

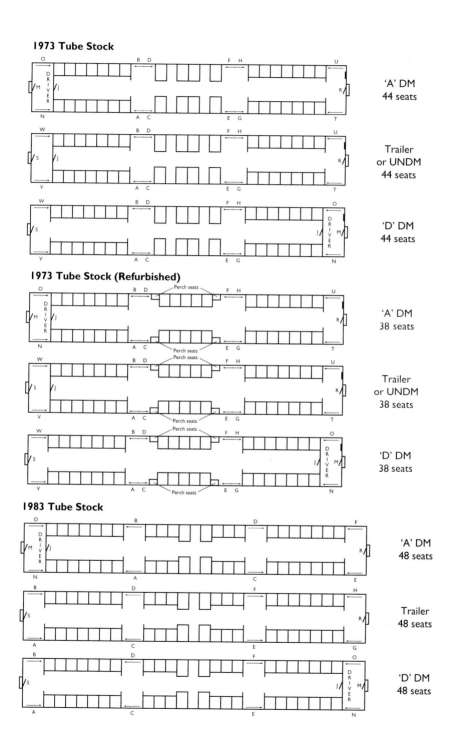

'A' DM
44 seats

Trailer
or UNDM
44 seats

'D' DM
44 seats

1973 Tube Stock (Refurbished)

'A' DM
38 seats

Trailer
or UNDM
38 seats

'D' DM
38 seats

1983 Tube Stock

'A' DM
48 seats

Trailer
48 seats

'D' DM
48 seats

1992 Tube Stock

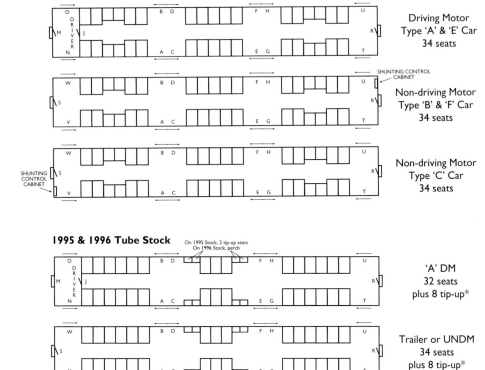

Driving Motor
Type 'A' & 'E' Car
34 seats

Non-driving Motor
Type 'B' & 'F' Car
34 seats

Non-driving Motor
Type 'C' Car
34 seats

1995 & 1996 Tube Stock

On 1995 Stock, 2 tip-up seats
On 1996 Stock, perch

'A' DM
32 seats
plus 8 tip-up*

Trailer or UNDM
34 seats
plus 8 tip-up*

'D' DM
32 seats
plus 8 tip-up*

On 1995 Tube Stock, the front cab 'M' door is a normal inward-opening door.
On 1996 Tube Stock, the front cab 'M' door lowers to form detraining steps.

* 1995 Stock only.

A60/62 Stock

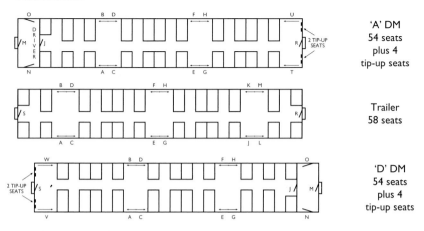

'A' DM
54 seats
plus 4
tip-up seats

Trailer
58 seats

'D' DM
54 seats
plus 4
tip-up seats

Note: On refurbished A stock operating outer end cabs, the 'J' door opens on the opposite side

C Stock - Refurbished

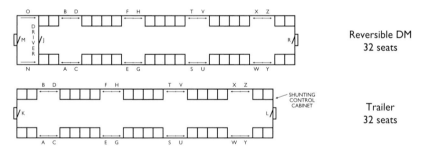

Reversible DM
32 seats

Trailer
32 seats

D Stock

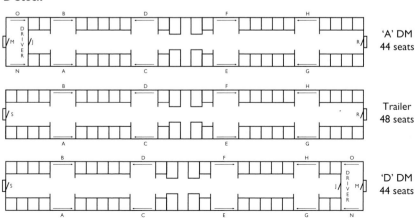

'A' DM
44 seats

Trailer
48 seats

'D' DM
44 seats

CARS RENUMBERED

For various reasons, some of the rolling stock in use on the Underground has been renumbered. This appendix gives details of the renumbering of all current stock. For the reasons for renumbering, please refer to the appropriate chapter.

1959 TUBE STOCK

Original No.	Renumbered	Date	Original No.	Renumbered	Date
1070	**1309R**	8. 77	1085	**1031R***	5. 88

* Renumbered 1031 in June 1990.

1960 TUBE STOCK

Original No.	Renumbered	Date	Renumbered	Date	Renumbered	Date
092392	A92392	2. 44	012392	10. 50	**4929**	2. 76

1962 TUBE STOCK

Original No.	Renumbered	Date	Original No.	Renumbered	Date
2452	**2522**	8. 83	2734	**2678**	5. 82
2510	**2570**	7. 83	9501	**9459**	5. 89
2728	**2682**	7. 83			

1967 TUBE STOCK

Original No.	Renumbered	Date	Original No.	Renumbered	Date
3116	**3016***	2. 95	3107	**3183**	2. 89
4116	**4016**	2. 95	4107	**4183**	2. 89
3101	**3180**	7. 88	3122	**3186**	7. 88
4101	**4180**	7. 88	4122	**4186**	7. 88
3103	**3181**	2. 89	3141	**3184**	10. 87
4103	**4181**	2. 89	4141	**4184**	10. 87
3105	**3182**	7. 88	3152	**3185**	5. 88
4105	**4182**	7. 88	4152	**4185**	5. 88

* The original 3016 exists awaiting scrapping.

1972 TUBE STOCK

Original No.	Renumbered	Date	Original No.	Renumbered	Date
3203	**3264**	2. 92	3527	**3081†**	2. 89
3204	**3116§**	2. 95	3529	**3105**	2. 89
3210	**3267**	6. 97	4203	**4264**	2. 92
3216	**3085**	5. 88	4204	**4116§**	2. 95
3217	**3080**	7. 88	4210	**4267**	6. 97
3218	**3265**	10. 94	4216	**4085**	5. 88
3220	**3086**	7. 88	4217	**4080**	7. 88
3223	**3082**	7. 88	4218	**4265**	10. 94
3225	**3083**	2. 89	4220	**4086**	7. 88

Original No.	Renumbered	Date	Original No.	Renumbered	Date
3303	3364	2. 92	4223	4082	7. 88
3310	3367	6. 97	4225	4083	2. 89
3316	3152	6. 88	4303	4364	2. 92
3317	3101	6. 88	4310	4367	6. 97
3318	3365	10. 94	4316	4152	6. 88
3320	3122	7. 88	4317	4101	6. 88
3323	3103	8. 88	4318	4365	10. 94
3324	3266†	6. 95	4320	4122	7. 88
3325	3107	2. 89	4323	4103	8. 88
3349	3366	6. 95	4324	4266†	6. 95
3401	3464	2. 92	4325	4107	2. 89
3407	3465	10. 94	4349	4366	6. 95
3412	3467	6. 97	4501	4564	2. 92
3424	3466	6. 95	4507	4565	10. 94
3501	3564	2. 92	4512	4567	6. 97
3507	3565	10. 94	4516	4141	6. 88
3512	3567	6. 97	4520	4084†	10. 87
3516	3141	6. 88	4524	4566	6. 95
3520	3084†	10. 87	4527	4081†	2. 89
3524	3566	6. 95	4529	4105	2. 89

† Converted from 'D' end to 'A' end.
§ Converted from 'A' end to 'D' end.

1973 TUBE STOCK

1983 TUBE STOCK

Original No.	Renumbered	Date	Original No.	Renumbered	Date
114	896	4. 93	3728	3730	1. 97
688	696	4. 93	3730	3728	1. 97
889	897	4. 93			

A60/62 STOCK

Original No.	Renumbered	Date	Original No.	Renumbered	Date
5008	5034	7. 85	5208	5218	8. 92
5009	5235	9. 94	5209	5121	3. 93
5028	5232	6. 85	6008	6234	9. 94
5034	5008*	7. 85	6009	6235	9. 94
5036	5116	4. 93	6028	6232	6. 85
5037	5117	4. 93	6037	6117	4. 93
5117	5233	8. 85	6117	6233	8. 85

* Further renumbered 5234 in September 1994.

D STOCK

Original No.	Renumbered	Date	Original No.	Renumbered	Date
17035	17077	12. 94	17077	17035	12. 94

The DLR station at Bank is deepest in the Bank station complex, being located under the Northern Line. A B.92 (ex-B.90 converted) unit is at the rear of an arriving train. *Brian Hardy*

DOCKLANDS LIGHT RAILWAY

Operating at 750V d.c. 3rd rail (underside contact), the initial sections of the Docklands Light Railway from Tower Gateway and Stratford to Island Gardens opened to the public on 31st August 1987, for which eleven light rail vehicles (numbered 01–11 and known as P. 86 stock) were built by Linke Hofmann Busch of Salzgitter, Germany. Each train comprises a two-body articulated unit with accommodation for two wheelchairs. Each articulated unit has four double doorways on each side which open and fold back inwards. The cars are finished in a two-tone red and blue livery, the red extending up and over the top of the doors. Apart from unit 07, which entered service on 2nd September 1987, all vehicles entered service on the opening day, 31st August 1987.

The Docklands Light Railway operates entirely automatically, being computer controlled from the system headquarters at Poplar, where the original depot is located. On board each train is a member of staff, a 'Train Captain', who is able to start the train from any doorway position. In the event of a problem, manual driving is possible by the Train Captain using controls in a 'desk' normally locked out of use at the outer ends of the vehicles.

The P.86 stock was not designed, nor was suitable, for tunnel running because when the initial railway was conceived no tunnel routes were planned. However, construction of an extension in twin tube tunnels from Royal Mint Street (east of Tower Gateway) to Bank commenced in March 1988. For passenger services to Bank, a second batch of ten vehicles (P.89 stock) was built by BREL of York. Numbered 12 to 21, these ten units were delivered to Poplar between December 1989 and May 1990. Unit 12 was the first to enter service on 11th May 1990, supplementing the original trains and enabling increased services to operate. The P.89 stock cars when new were very similar to their older P.86 counterparts and although only a small number of minor detail differences exist between them, the P.89 stock was built to operate in tunnel conditions.

An interior view of a B stock unit, looking towards the centre articulated section. *Brian Hardy*

In addition to providing an extension to Bank, it was also desirable to operate two-unit trains whenever possible and with a further extension from Poplar east to Beckton given the go-ahead, more new stock was required. A total of 70 articulated units were ordered from BN Constructions Ferrovaires et Metalliques of Brugge in Belgium. The first batch, known as B.90 stock and fitted with the then existing signalling equipment, comprised 23 vehicles (22–44). The B stock trains differ from their P stock sisters by having sliding doors mounted outside the carbody and have a redesigned front end with centre access. There are 66 seats per vehicle (plus four tip-up seats), but with more longitudinal seating than with the P type.

The first B.90 unit (22) arrived on 31st January 1991 and entered service on 1st July 1991. The extension to Bank was opened on 29th July 1991, at first using the westbound tunnel only, double-line operation commencing on 29th November 1991. The B.90 stock thus complemented the existing vehicles to provide the service between from Bank, Tower Gateway and Stratford to Island Gardens. The P.86 trains were banned from running to Bank and always worked singly, but two-unit operation (of both P.89 and B.90 types, but never mixed) commenced from 25th February 1991, although rather spasmodically to start with.

B.92 unit 51 heads an eastbound train into East India on the Beckton branch. The B.90 and B.92 types are indistinguishable. *Brian Hardy*

The remainder of the B stock fleet (47 vehicles numbered 45–91) is classed as B.92 stock and from new has been fitted with Alcatel signalling equipment, although in other respects it is identical in appearance to the B.90 stock. One of the B.90 stock cars (35) was delivered in August 1991 fitted with Alcatel signalling for test purposes, along with the first two B.92 units (45–46) in October 1991. The remainder of the B.92 stock was delivered direct to the new Beckton depot between March 1992 and March 1993. Opening of the Beckton extension was achieved on 28th March 1994, initially as a shuttle service to and from Poplar, with through services to Tower Gateway from 31st July 1995.

Cosmetic changes to DLR rolling stock have seen LT-style 'Light Rail' roundels applied from June 1991, indicating LRT's ownership of the system, but with the transfer of control from LRT to the LDDC on 1st April 1992, these were hastily removed in March 1992. The cars then continued with their original signing and numbers until March 1993, when a new Docklands 'Light Rail' logo was introduced. In November 1995 B.92 unit 45 appeared in service in corporate DLR livery of petrol blue and grey, being a trial with self-adhesive vinyl film over the original colours. B.92 (converted ex-B.90) unit 32 has had an interior modernisation to generate more standing space, at the expense of ten seats in each centre bay.

Construction began in September 1996 of a further extension of the DLR, to take the southern leg in tunnel under the River Thames to terminate at Lewisham.

The new Alcatel signalling system was introduced on the DLR in stages, first on the Beckton extension, followed by Stratford – Canary Wharf on 18th April 1995, and the rest of the railway on 10th July 1995. From this latter date, the P.89 and remaining P.86 units became superfluous, being unable to operate on the new system. Whilst the B.90 cars have subsequently been converted to match their B.92 counterparts, the P.86 cars were purchased by Essen Verkehrs AG (EVAG) in Germany in 1991. Between 1991 and 1995, the cars made their way back to Germany to their new owners. The same company also purchased the P.89 cars in 1996 and, to date, five out of the ten cars have departed the DLR.

DLR Rolling Stock as at mid-June 1997 was as follows:

P. 89 Stock (BREL) – Awaiting transfer to Essen 5
15* 16 18* 19 20

B. 90 Stock (BN) – converted ex-B. 90 23
22 23 24 25 26 27 28 29 30 31 32§ 33 34 35‡ 36 37 38 39 40 41
42 43 44

B. 92 Stock (BN) 47
45† 46 47 48 49 50 51 52 53 54 55 56 57 58 59 60 61 62 63 64
65 66 67 68 69 70 71 72 73 74 75 76 77 78 79 80 81 82 83 84
85 86 87 88 89 90 91

* Following collision on 22nd April 1991, units 15 and 18 were reformed and renumbered. The damaged cars 15 ('B' end) and 18 ('A' end) are now unit 15. Unit 18 thus comprises the 'A' end of the original unit 15.
§ Interior layout altered in 1996.
† Unit in petrol blue and grey livery.
‡ B. 92 prototype unit.

A two-unit train of 1980 'Greenbat' stock stands in Paddington station, awaiting departure.
Brian Hardy

POST OFFICE RAILWAY

Construction of the Post Office Tube railway was begun in 1915, but because of the First World War it was another 12 years before the first section was opened. This was on 5th December 1927 between Paddington and Mount Pleasant, the next section opening eastwards to Liverpool Street on 28th December 1927. The final section to Eastern District Office at Whitechapel opened on 2nd January 1928. This non-passenger carrying railway at first conveyed only parcels until 13th February 1928, from when letters were carried as well. The railway is 6.44 miles in length and the 2ft gauge tracks are generally in double-track tube tunnels of 9ft diameter, separating at station approaches into single tube tunnels of 7ft diameter. The driverless trains operate on a centre 3rd rail system at either 150V d.c. in station areas, or at 440V d.c. between stations, allowing speeds of about 7mph and 35 mph respectively. The automatic operation of the trains is controlled by track circuits. One of the running rails is bonded to earth and acts as a common return for both traction and track circuiting. The other rail is, electrically, a series of individual lengths insulated from each other. When the wheels of a train bridge the rails, the relay connected to that particular track circuit operates, removing power from the preceding section and not restoring it until the train has moved onto the next section. The train brakes operate in the absence of traction current and thus the system is fail-safe. At stations, train movements were until 1993 controlled manually from a switch frame, which was mechanically and electrically interlocked. Trains could thus be shunted or manually routed through. A new computerised signalling system was installed on the railway, replacing the manually-operated switch cabins at stations. Commissioned in station-by-station stages from east to west from 13th June 1993, the last stage was completed on 25th July 1993 at Paddington.

One of the retained units of 1930–36 stock in red livery stands on the depot ramp access tracks in Mount Pleasant depot. *Brian Hardy*

Because of the opening of the new Willesden Distribution Centre, which handles most of the mail in the London area, the role of the Post Office railway has declined and reductions in services from 30th September 1996 resulted in the railway operating for 18 hours a day, from 13.00 to 07.00, the six-hour break being utilised for maintenance purposes. Major engineering and maintenance work is undertaken when the line closes at 07.00 on Saturday until 13.00 Monday. Just four operational stations remain – Paddington, Rathbone Place, Mount Pleasant and Whitechapel Eastern District Office. One or two units per train operate according to traffic requirements and the normal 5-minute interval service is supplemented with additional trains as traffic demands. The trains are serviced and maintained at the depot at Mount Pleasant, which is connected to the main running lines by a steeply graded incline.

For the opening of the railway, 90 four-wheel cars were built by the Kilmarnock Engineering Company with equipment by English Electric, and were designed to operate in three-vehicle formation. These cars were not successful and were replaced between 1930 and 1931 by 50 bogie cars from English Electric, being numbered 752–763 and 793–830, the first entering service singly in May 1930. Two-car operation with these new cars commenced on 9th September 1930. A further ten similar cars (923–932) were delivered in 1936 because of increasing postal traffic. These 60 cars thus provided the daily service very reliably over the next 45 years or more. The mail containers, however, originally built of plywood, were replaced by aluminium containers in the 1950s following experiments in 1948.

Two prototype trains were built by English Electric in 1962, entering service in 1964. No further examples were built and one was scrapped in 1973, the other being withdrawn in 1980. To replace the bulk of the 1930–36 stock, 34 new cars numbered 501–534 were built by Greenbat of Leeds and were delivered to the railway at Mount Pleasant between 1980 and 1982. In addition, two end bogies were provided as spares (both numbered 535) to replace fellow motor ends when necessary. From new the new cars were painted in Post Office red, unlike their predecessors, which were in pale green. Two older cars however (801 and 806) were repainted into 'gold' livery in 1977 to celebrate the railway's Golden Jubilee.

In addition to the 34 new Greenbat cars, 17 of the 1930–36 type were retained, refurbished and subsequently returned to service in 1985–86. These were repainted in Post Office red to match the Greenbat cars. Three of these cars have been converted with a new design of ramp lowering device, of the type fitted to the Greenbat cars. The remaining 1962 prototype was also returned to service in 1986 by salvaging equipment from the previously withdrawn pair, bearing the fleet number 66.

To enable the trains to be compatible with the new computer system, all operational trains (apart from prototype car 66) were renumbered from the end of September 1992. Former numbers are shown in the list below. The old 1930–36 stock cars stored at various locations and the spare Greenbat bogies have not been renumbered. In addition, the fleet of 1930–36 cars has been reduced by two, to 15.

1980 Greenbat 35

01 (501)	02 (502)	03 (503)	04 (504)	05 (505)	06 (506)	07 (507)	08 (508)
09 (509)	10 (510)	11 (511)	12 (512)	13 (513)	14 (514)	15 (515)	16 (516)
17 (517)	18 (518)	19 (519)	20 (520)	21 (521)	22 (522)	23 (523)	24 (524)
25 (525)	26 (526)	27 (527)	28 (528)	29 (529)	30 (530)	31 (531)	32 (532)
33 (533)	34 (534)	†535					

† 535 comprises two single motor bogies (spare)

1930–31 English Electric 13

35 (755)	36 (756)	37 (760)	38 (761)	39 (762)	*41 (805)	42 (806)	43 (811)
44 (812)	45 (814)	47 (819)	48 (824)	49 (827)			

* 805 body ex-817 in 1981

1936 English Electric 2

50 (928)   51 (931)

1926 Battery Cars 3

1   2   3

The following cars are preserved:

601   Mount Pleasant Workshop – 1927 4-wheeled stock.
803   Buckinghamshire Railway Centre, Quainton Road – 1930/31 English Electric.
807   Science Museum – 1930/31 English Electric.
808   West Somerset Railway, Minehead – 1930/31 English Electric.
809   National Railway Museum, York – 1930/31 English Electric.

Cars stored out of service 21

Rathbone Place:	752	759	763	793	795	799	802	804	813
	816	817	818	820	822	826	830	925	932
Wimpole Street:	797								
Liverpool Street:	66	810							

2558 is one of two ERF EC8 dustcarts in the fleet, the only vehicles of this chassis make in stock. Three other dustcarts are owned, these being on Mercedes-Benz chassis. *Capital Transport*

LUL DISTRIBUTION SERVICES

On 1st April 1989 Distribution Services was transferred from the direct control of London Regional Transport to become a wholly-owned subsidiary of London Underground Limited. The origins of the fleet go back to 1933, when the newly-formed London Passenger Transport Board inherited a varied collection of ancillary and support vehicles from its predecessors. From 1st November 1939 vehicles were numbered in a common series starting from 1, with chassis type or purpose denoted by a suffix letter; and in October 1949 the Central Distribution Services was formed to take responsibility for the service vehicle fleet of London Transport's various departments.

The original numbering system continues in use to this day, although an additional 3000+ series for leased vehicles commenced in 1982. Recently, with the computerisation of fleet records, many lorries and vans can be seen without their fleet number suffixes, and it has been suggested their use might be discontinued. Indeed, at the time of writing, no suffix letter had yet been chosen for the two ERF dustcarts which joined the fleet in 1996.

From 1990, the former red and grey LT liveries, and the short-lived use of all-over blue on LUL vans, were all replaced by a new white colour scheme based on the 1989 LUL corporate rolling stock livery, with vehicle skirts, dropsides and tail-boards finished in blue. Vehicles bear the Underground roundel and are generally lettered 'Engineering services' or 'Support services' in blue as appropriate; though vans and lorries operated by the LUL Emergency Response Unit carry the ERU title together with distinctive red and blue frontal chevron stripes.

Mercedes-Benz 410D vans 2530M (leading) and 2531M represent the medium-sized vehicles used by LUL's Emergency Response Unit, and exhibit the distinctive red and blue chevrons unique to this department. They are seen here in Lower Regent Street on 4th December 1996, whilst attending a derailment at Piccadilly Circus. *Kim Rennie*

2492M is a larger Mercedes truck with a demountable container interchangeable with other similar vehicles. It is seen at the top of Whitehall in March 1997. *Colin Lloyd*

A number of cars, vans and minibuses continue to be supplied to London Transport Buses, the organisation now responsible for the operation and maintenance of bus stations, stops and stands, as well as the implementation of planned and emergency route diversions. These are usually finished in a white livery and are lettered 'London Transport Buses' and 'Operating Services' in black and red respectively, with plain LT roundels coloured white on a red square. A few LTB cars remain in a previous all-red scheme and have white logos. Also, some LUL and LTB vehicles can be seen in white, with no other identification apart from a blue or black fleet number.

The composition of the Distribution Services fleet has been affected by the changes undergone by the parent London Transport organisation as a whole. The abolition of roadside bus route supervision saw the demise of the final generation of inspectors' radio cars/vans, and the Leyland Freighter recovery trucks have been disposed of, in many cases sold to the bus companies that formerly operated them. For the most part, vehicles allocated to the Docklands Light Railway, LTA/TDI Advertising and the London Buses subsidiaries continued in use following transfer or privatisation, and until their individual leasing contracts with Distribution Services expired.

Though the fleet was standardised on Fords for many years, a more diverse procurement policy is followed nowadays. Heavier vehicles tend to be owned and are mainly based on Mercedes-Benz chassis. Smaller types such as cars, vans and mini-buses are normally leased and replaced on a more regular basis, with Ford and Vauxhall types predominating; although recently a sizeable number of Volkswagen Transporter vans have been introduced for use by LTB.

2552 is one of two Mercedes articulated tractor units purchased in 1995, seen here coupled to a low loader at Acton Works. *Capital Transport*

Unlike days gone by, specialised vehicle types tend to be few and far between, with most lorries and vans being bought 'off the peg' to standard manufacturers' designs. Notable in today's fleet though are 2488M, the LUL communications and control unit; 4404LR, a high-voltage mains fault investigation Land Rover with custom body; and 4687F, a newly-acquired Ford Transit mobile information office for LTB complete with 'ice cream van' style high-top bodywork and nearside sliding window. The distinctive pair of tall-bodied uniform distribution trailers that replaced the last Ford D1010 mobile uniform issue units in 1993 are currently out of use and in store at Acton, following a change of policy regarding LUL clothing issue. A small number of other 'one off' types have also been brought into stock recently, and may influence future orders.

Land Rover 4404LR (erroneously missing the "R" of its fleet number suffix) is a unique custom-bodied vehicle based at 10A Wood Lane, W12; and used for High Voltage mains fault investigation work. Illustrating the plain white livery worn by a few Distribution Services vehicles, the unit visits Neasden Depot substation on 21st December 1996. *Kim Rennie*

DISTRIBUTION SERVICES FLEET

Stock No.	Reg. No.	Chassis type	Body	Date in Stock
OWNED VEHICLES				
1282F	580 EYU	Ford Thames 3 ton van	Auxiliary breakdown tender	1963*
2407F	A407 SJD	Ford Cargo 1613	Dropside lorry	1985
2422L	B561 YYN	Freight Rover Sherpa 350SL	Van + tow-bar	1985
2435L	D295 ECR	Leyland Freighter T45	Dropside lorry	1986
2457B	D66 ALO	Bedford Midi-Van	Van	1986
2464L	E693 GLT	Leyland Freighter 1313	Dropside lorry + crew-cab/tail-lift	1988
2471M	D543 CLC	Mercedes-Benz 1625	Articulated tractor unit	1988
2472M	G384 VJB	Mercedes-Benz 1617	Articulated tractor unit	1989
2474M	G227 YLT	Mercedes-Benz 1726	Articulated tractor unit	1990
2478M	G924 ALM	Mercedes-Benz 408D	Demountable lorry	1990
2480M	G926 ALM	Mercedes-Benz 408D	Demountable lorry	1990
2482M	H327 FLH	Mercedes-Benz 2421	Dustcart	1990
2483M	H329 FLH	Mercedes-Benz 2421	Dustcart	1990
2484M	G794 BLM	Mercedes-Benz 609D	Highroof van	1990
2487M	H218 FLB	Mercedes-Benz 814	Dropside lorry	1990
2488M	H219 FLB	Mercedes-Benz 814	LUL communications unit 'Jim Winters MBE'	1991
2489M	H220 HLB	Mercedes-Benz 814	Dropside lorry	1990
2490M	H221 FLB	Mercedes-Benz 814	Box truck + tail-lift	1990
2491M	H223 FLB	Mercedes-Benz 1114	Demountable equipment truck	1990
2492M	H224 FLB	Mercedes-Benz 1114	Demountable equipment truck	1990
2493M	H225 FLB	Mercedes-Benz 1114	Demountable equipment truck	1990
2494M	H226 FLB	Mercedes-Benz 1114	Demountable equipment truck	1990
2495M	H437 GAN	Mercedes-Benz 1114	Demountable equipment truck	1990
2496M	H438 GAN	Mercedes-Benz 1114	Demountable equipment truck	1990
2498F	H208 FLM	Ford Cargo 1313	Dropside lorry + crew-cab/tail-lift/winch	1990
2499F	H219 FLM	Ford Cargo 1313	Dropside lorry + crew-cab/tail-lift/winch	1990
2502F	K251 PLA	Ford Transit	15-seat minibus	1992
2503F	K252 PLA	Ford Transit	15-seat minibus	1992
2504M	K672 PLH	Mercedes-Benz 410D	Tipper truck	1992
2506F	K157 PLY	Ford Transit	15-seat minibus	1992
2507F	K158 PLY	Ford Transit 190	High-top van	1993
2508M	K490 RLA	Mercedes-Benz 1114	Demountable truck	1993
2509M	K489 RLA	Mercedes-Benz 1114	Demountable truck	1993
2510M	K461 RLA	Mercedes-Benz 410D	Curtainsided truck	1993
2511M	K462 RLA	Mercedes-Benz 410D	Curtainsided truck	1993
2522F	K221 RLO	Ford Cargo 170	Dropside lorry	1993
2523F	K229 RLO	Ford Cargo 170	Dropside lorry	1993
2524F	K245 RLO	Ford Cargo 170	Dropside lorry	1993
2525M	K479 RLA	Mercedes-Benz 1520	Articulated tractor unit	1993
2526M	K480 RLA	Mercedes-Benz 1520	Articulated tractor unit	1993
2527M	K477 RLA	Mercedes-Benz 1520	Articulated tractor unit	1993
2528M	K478 RLA	Mercedes-Benz 1520	Articulated tractor unit	1993
2529M	K407 SLB	Mercedes-Benz 410D	Van + crew-cab	1993
2530M	L87 ULA	Mercedes-Benz 410D	Van + crew-cab	1993
2531M	L85 ULA	Mercedes-Benz 410D	Van + crew-cab	1993
2532M	L129 ULA	Mercedes-Benz 410D	Van + crew-cab	1993
2534M	K491 RLA	Mercedes-Benz 1114	Demountable lorry	1993
2535F	K273 RLO	Ford Cargo 130	Dropside lorry + crew-cab	1993
2536M	K387 RLR	Mercedes-Benz 1114	Demountable lorry	1993
2537M	K492 RLA	Mercedes-Benz 1114	Demountable lorry	1993
2538M	K397 RLR	Mercedes-Benz 2422	Tipper truck	1993
2539M	K387 SLB	Mercedes-Benz 410D	Dropside lorry	1993
2540M	K388 RLR	Mercedes-Benz 1114	Demountable lorry	1993
2541M	K396 RLR	Mercedes-Benz 410D	Demountable lorry	1993
2542M	K119 DCF	Mercedes-Benz 410D	Tipper truck + crew-cab	1993
2543M	K120 DCF	Mercedes-Benz 308D	Dropside lorry	1993
2544M	K121 DCF	Mercedes-Benz 308D	Dropside lorry	1993
2545M	K396 SLB	Mercedes-Benz 410D	Dropside lorry + crew-cab	1993
2546M	K275 RLO	Ford Cargo 110	Demountable equipment truck	1993
2547F	K274 RLO	Ford Cargo 110	Demountable equipment truck	1993
2548F	L339 WLF	Ford Transit 190	Mini-tipper	1994
2549F	L340 WLF	Ford Transit 190	Van	1994
2550F	K495 RLA	Ford Escort 1.8D	Van	1993
2551	M25DLN	Mercedes-Benz 2534	Articulated tractor unit	1995
2552	M24DLN	Mercedes-Benz 1520	Articulated tractor unit	1995
2553M	N614 FLA	Mercedes-Benz 1820	Dropside lorry	1995
2555F	N589 FLE	Ford Cargo	Demountable lorry	1995
2556M	N930 HLT	Mercedes-Benz 814	Dustcart	1996
2557	P966 FKN	ERF EC8	Dustcart	1996
2558	P967 FKN	ERF EC8	Dustcart	1996
LEASED VEHICLES				
4196F	K601 OBY	Ford Transit 190	Dropside lorry + double cab/tail-lift	1992
4199F	J152 NLD	Ford Transit 160	17-seat crewbus	1992
4200F	J151 NLD	Ford Transit 160	17-seat crewbus	1992

4219F	K889 XVS	Ford Transit	Van	1993
4256F	K785 FWE	Ford Transit 190	Van + crew-cab	1993
4250F	K781 FWE	Ford Transit 100	Van	1993
4264F	K902 XVS	Ford Escort 40	Van	1992
4267F	K942 XVS	Ford Escort 40	Van	1993
4269F	K792 FWE	Ford P100 1.8	Pick-up truck	1993
4271F	K794 FWE	Ford Escort 1.8LD	Van	1993
4272F	K795 FWE	Ford Escort 1.8LD	Van	1993
4277B	K986 PVK	Vauxhall Astra 1.4iLS	Van	1993
4279B	K574 NPO	Vauxhall Astra 1.4LS	5-door estate car	1992
4280B	K573 NPO	Vauxhall Astra 1.4LS	5-door estate car	1992
4281F	K799 FWE	Ford Fiesta 1.8D	Van	1992
4289F	K922 AJW	Ford Transit 190	Dropside lorry + double cab	1992
4297F	K864 NAB	Ford Escort 1.4LS	5-door estate car	1993
4305F	K548 BPP	Ford Escort 1.8LD	5-door estate car	1993
4306F	K541 BPP	Ford Escort 1.8LD	5-door estate car	1993
4307F	K547 BPP	Ford Escort 1.8LD	5-door estate car	1993
4308F	K886 BBH	Ford Escort 40 1.8LD	Van	1993
4309V	K674 YOL	Volkswagen Transporter 1.9	Van	1993
4310V	K664 YOL	Volkswagen Transporter 1.9	Van	1993
4311V	K673 YOL	Volkswagen Transporter 1.9	Van	1993
4313V	K675 YOL	Volkswagen Transporter 1.9	Van	1993
4314V	K964 YBL	Volkswagen Transporter 1.9	Van	1993
4315V	K965 YBL	Volkswagen Transporter 1.9	Van	1993
4317V	K967 YBL	Volkswagen Transporter 1.9	Van	1993
4332F	L753 HFU	Ford Transit 190	Van	1993
4349F	L825 HFU	Ford Escort 40 1.8	Van	1993
4350F	L752 HFU	Ford Transit 190 LWB	Van	1993
4352F	L538 FUR	Ford Escort 1.8LD	5-door estate car	1993
4353F	L588 FUR	Ford Escort 1.8LD	5-door estate car	1993
4356B	L284 CJX	Vauxhall Astramax 1.7D	Van	1993
4363F	L679 LHL	Ford Transit 190	Dropside lorry + double cab	1993
4364F	L756 HFU	Ford Transit 190	Van	1993
4365B	L798 BPL	Vauxhall Astra 1.4 Merit	Van	1993
4366F	L348 APK	Ford Escort 1.8LD	5-door estate car	1993
4367B	L953 BPG	Vauxhall Astra 1.4LS	5-door estate car	1993
4368F	L715 NWB	Ford Transit 190	Dropside lorry + double cab	1994
4369F	L714 NWB	Ford Transit 190	Dropside lorry + double cab	1994
4373F	L861 HFU	Ford Transit 190	Van	1993
4374F	L617 JEE	Ford Transit 100	Van	1994
4375F	L610 JEE	Ford Transit 100	Van	1994
4376F	L609 JEE	Ford Transit 100	Van	1994
4377F	L611 JEE	Ford Transit 190	Van	1994
4378F	L860 HFU	Ford Escort 1.8LD	Van	1993
4379F	L862 HFU	Ford Transit 190	Van + crew-cab	1993
4380B	L279 MKY	Vauxhall Astra 1.4i Merit Auto	4-door saloon car	1994
4381V	L982 OWA	Volkswagen Transporter 1.9	Van	1994
4382F	L713 NWB	Ford Transit 190	Dropside lorry + double cab	1994
4383V	L976 OWA	Volkswagen Transporter 1.9	Van	1994
4384V	L977 OWA	Volkswagen Transporter 1.9	Van	1994
4385V	L978 OWA	Volkswagen Transporter 1.9	Van	1994
4386V	L979 OWA	Volkswagen Transporter 1.9	Van	1994
4387V	L980 OWA	Volkswagen Transporter 1.9	Van	1994
4388V	L981 OWA	Volkswagen Transporter 1.9	Van	1994
4390B	L259 MKY	Vauxhall Astra 1.7LSD	5-door estate car	1994
4391B	L146 MKY	Vauxhall Midi 2.2 SWB	Van	1993
4392F	L603 JEE	Ford Transit 190	Dropside lorry + double cab	1994
4393F	L602 JEE	Ford Transit	12-seat minibus	1994
4394F	L601 JEE	Ford Transit 190	Van	1994
4398F	L619 JEE	Ford Transit 100	Van	1994
4399F	L592 JFU	Ford Transit 190	Van	1994
4400F	L768 JFU	Ford Transit 150 LWB	Van	1994
4401LR	L672 NBH	Land Rover 110	12-seat station wagon crewbus	1994
4402LR	L673 NBH	Land Rover 110	12-seat station wagon crewbus	1994
4403F	L767 JFU	Ford Transit 190	Van	1994
4404LR	M997 BEC	Land Rover 110 TDI LWB	H. V. mains fault investigation unit	1994
4405F	L948 NEH	Ford Transit 100	Van	1994
4406F	L947 NEH	Ford Transit 100	Van	1994
4407F	L949 NEH	Ford Transit 100	Van	1994
4409F	L463 WLF	Ford Transit 100	Van	1994
4411F	L461 WLF	Ford Transit 100	Van	1994
4412F	L460 WLF	Ford Transit 100	Van	1994
4413F	L459 WLF	Ford Transit 100	Van	1994
4414F	L759 NWB	Ford Transit 190	Dropside lorry + double cab	1994
4415F	L961 KBE	Ford Transit 100	Van	1994
4416B	L413 OKU	Vauxhall Astra 1.6iLS	Van	1994
4417B	M41 SKY	Vauxhall Astra 1.6iLS	Van	1994
4418B	L396 OKU	Vauxhall Astra 1.4L 2+2	Van	1994
4419F	L947 KBE	Ford Transit 190	Van	1994
4420F	M308 TDT	Ford Transit 190	Van	1994
4421F	M306 TDT	Ford Transit 190	Van	1994

4422F	M505 LJV	Ford Transit 190	Van	1994
4423F	M506 LJV	Ford Transit 190	Van	1994
4424F	L950 KBE	Ford Transit 190	Van	1994
4426F	M309 TDT	Ford Transit 190	Van	1994
4427F	M307 TDT	Ford Transit 190	Van	1994
4428F	M497 LJV	Ford Transit 190	Van	1994
4429F	M507 LJV	Ford Transit 190	Van	1994
4430F	M310 TDT	Ford Transit 190	Dropside lorry + double cab	1994
4431F	M168 SRE	Ford Transit 100	Van	1994
4432F	M665 LJV	Ford Transit 100	Van	1994
4433F	L955 KBE	Ford Transit 190	Van	1994
4434F	M311 TDT	Ford Transit 190	Van	1994
4435F	M708 LJV	Ford Transit 100	Van	1994
4436F	L670 PBF	Ford Transit 100	Van	1994
4437F	L956 KBE	Ford Transit 190	Van	1994
4438F	M167 SRE	Ford Transit 100	Van	1994
4439F	M749 LJV	Ford Transit	12-seat semi-highroof minibus	1994
4440F	M647 OPP	Ford Escort 1. 8LD	5-door estate car	1994
4441F	M501 LJV	Ford Escort 1. 8	Van	1994
4442F	M498 LJV	Ford Escort 1. 8	Van	1994
4443F	M499 LJV	Ford Escort 1. 8	Van	1994
4444F	M503 LJV	Ford Escort 1. 8	Van	1994
4445F	M502 LJV	Ford Escort 1. 8	Van	1994
4446F	L958 KBE	Ford Escort 1. 8	Van	1994
4447F	L959 KBE	Ford Escort 1. 8	Van	1994
4448B	L874 PWA	Vauxhall Astra 1. 4iLS	5-door estate car	1994
4449F	M645 OPP	Ford Escort 1. 8LD	5-door estate car	1994
4450F	M646 OPP	Ford Escort 1. 8LD	5-door estate car	1994
4451F	L967 KBE	Ford Transit 150 LWB	Van	1994
4452F	M658 LJV	Ford Fiesta 1. 8LXD	Van	1994
4453F	M659 LJV	Ford Fiesta 1. 8LXD	Van	1994
4454F	L960 KBE	Ford Escort 1. 8D	Van	1994
4455F	L965 KBE	Ford Transit 100	Van	1994
4456F	L957 KBE	Ford Transit 190	Van	1994
4457F	M568 LJV	Ford Transit	12-seat minibus	1994
4460F	L669 PBF	Ford Transit 100	Van	1994
4461F	M233 TEH	Ford Transit 190	High-top van	1994
4462F	M613 LJV	Ford Transit 190	Van	1995
4463F	M295 TDT	Ford Transit 190	Dropside lorry + double cab	1995
4464F	M265 FDG	Ford Escort 1. 8D	Van	1995
4465F	M56 MJV	Ford Transit	15-seat minibus	1995
4466F	M671 LJV	Ford Escort 1. 8D	Van	1994
4467F	M711 LJV	Ford Escort 1. 8D	Van	1994
4468V	M232 SAN	Volkswagen Transporter 2. 4i	Van	1995
4469V	M233 SAN	Volkswagen Transporter 2. 4i	Van	1995
4470V	M234 SAN	Volkswagen Transporter 2. 4i	Van	1995
4472F	M215 UEH	Ford Transit 100	Van	1994
4473F	M253 UEH	Ford Transit 100	Van	1995
4475F	M942 MFU	Ford Transit 100	Van	1994
4477T	M629 DHY	Toyota Previa 2. 4GL	5-door 'multi-purpose vehicle'	1995
4479B	N73 DBP	Vauxhall Frontera	5-door 4x4 'off the road' vehicle	1995
4480F	M845 NBE	Ford Transit 190	Van	1995
4484F	M779 MJV	Ford Transit 100 LWB	Van	1995
4485F	M829 TTM	Ford Courier 1. 8D	Van	1995
4486F	M802 MJV	Ford Escort 1. 8D	Van	1995
4487F	M367 CAH	Ford Transit 100	Van	1995
4488F	M803 MJV	Ford Transit 100	Van	1995
4489F	M801 MJV	Ford Transit 1. 8D	Van	1995
4490F	M847 NBE	Ford Transit 190	Van	1995
4491F	M849 NBE	Ford Transit 190	Van	1995
4492F	M840 NBE	Ford Transit 190	Dropside lorry + crew-cab	1995
4493F	M841 NBE	Ford Transit 190	Dropside lorry + crew-cab/tail-lift	1995
4494F	M850 NBE	Ford Transit 190	Van	1995
4495F	M851 NBE	Ford Transit 190	Van	1995
4496B	M901 MPE	Vauxhall Astra 1. 6LS	Van	1995
4497F	M584 NEE	Ford Transit 190	Van	1995
4499F	M664 TTM	Ford Fiesta 1. 8D	Van	1995
4500F	M665 TTM	Ford Fiesta 1. 8D	Van	1995
4502V	M371 TCF	Volkswagen Transporter	Van	1995
4503F	M566 NEE	Ford Escort 1. 8D	Van	1995
4504F	M565 NEE	Ford Escort 1. 8D	Van	1995
4505F	M564 NEE	Ford Escort 1. 8D	Van	1995
4506V	M374 TCF	Volkswagen Transporter 1. 9D	Van	1995
4507V	M373 TCF	Volkswagen Transporter 1. 9D	Van	1995
4509F	M585 NEE	Ford Transit 190 LWB	Van	1995
4510F	N26 PBE	Ford Transit 190 LWB	Van	1995
4511B	N968 RPM	Vauxhall Midi 2. 2. SWB	Van	1995
4512B	M899 MPE	Vauxhall Astra 1. 6iLS	Van	1995
4513B	M897 MPE	Vauxhall Astra 1. 6iLS	Van	1995
4514B	M898 MPE	Vauxhall Astra 1. 6iLS	Van	1995
4515B	M896 MPE	Vauxhall Astra 1. 6iLS	Van	1995

4516B	M895 MPE	Vauxhall Astra 1. 6iLS	Van	1995
4517B	M894 MPE	Vauxhall Astra 1. 6iLS	Van	1995
4518B	M892 MPE	Vauxhall Astra 1. 6iLS	Van	1995
4519B	M893 MPE	Vauxhall Astra 1. 6iLS	Van	1995
4520B	M891 MPE	Vauxhall Astra 1. 6iLS	Van	1995
4521B	M890 MPE	Vauxhall Astra 1. 6iLS	Van	1995
4522B	M889 MPE	Vauxhall Astra 1. 6iLS	Van	1995
4524F	M886 MBE	Ford Transit	12-seat minibus	1995
4527LR	M291 UWG	Land Rover 110	12-seat station wagon crewbus	1995
4528F	M595 NEE	Ford Transit 100	Van	1995
4529F	M186 NFU	Ford Courier	Van	1995
4530F	N56 PBE	Ford Transit 100	Van	1995
4531F	M562 UNK	Ford Escort 1. 8LD	5-door estate car	1995
4532F	N110 PBE	Ford Transit 190	Dropside lorry + double cab/tail-lift	1995
4533F	N109 PBE	Ford Transit 190	Dropside lorry + double cab/tail-lift	1995
4534F	N256 HGP	Ford Transit 190	Dropside lorry + double cab/tail-lift	1995
4535F	M752 OAC	Ford Escort 1. 4LX	5-door estate car	1995
4536F	N236 CTM	Ford Mondeo 1. 8LX Auto	5-door estate car	1995
4537F	N112 PBE	Ford Transit 190	Dropside lorry	1995
4538F	M297 LPM	Ford Escort 1. 8LD	5-door estate car	1995
4539F	N517 PJV	Ford Transit 190	Van	1996
4540F	N457 RBE	Ford Transit 190	Dropside lorry + tail-lift	1996
4541F	N41 PBE	Ford Transit 150 LWB	Van	1995
4542F	N492 PJV	Ford Transit 150 LWB	Van	1996
4543F	N493 PJV	Ford Transit 150 LWB	Van	1996
4544F	N491 PJV	Ford Transit 150 LWB	Van	1996
4545F	N490 PJV	Ford Transit 150 LWB	Van	1996
4546F	N488 PJV	Ford Transit 150 LWB	Van	1996
4547F	N457 RBE	Ford Transit 100	Van	1996
4548F	N86 PBE	Ford Transit	15-seat minibus	1995
4549F	N483 RBE	Ford Escort 1. 8LXD	Van	1996
4550F	N131 PBE	Ford Escort 1. 8D	Van	1996
4551F	N482 RBE	Ford Escort 1. 8D	Van	1995
4552B	N324 OYE	Vauxhall Astra 1. 7LSD	5-door estate car	1995
4553B	N235 EOR	Vauxhall Astra 2. 3L Auto	Van	1995
4554B	N247 EOR	Vauxhall Astra 1. 6GLSi	5-door estate car	1995
4555B	N182 FBP	Vauxhall Astra 1. 6GLSi	5-door estate car	1996
4556F	N489 PJV	Ford Transit 150 LWB	Van	1996
4557F	N370 PFU	Ford Transit 100	Van + crew-cab	1996
4558F	N151 PBE	Ford Transit 100	Van	1995
4559F	N149 PBE	Ford Escort 55D	Van	1995
4560F	N150 PBE	Ford Escort 55D	Van	1995
4561F	N462 PEE	Ford Escort 35	Van	1995
4562F	N764 GVF	Ford Transit 100	Van	1995
4563F	N763 GVF	Ford Transit 100	Van	1995
4564F	N463 PEE	Ford Escort 1. 8D	Van	1995
4565F	N377 PFU	Ford Transit	15-seat minibus	1996
4566F	N369 PFU	Ford Transit 190	Dropside lorry + crew-cab/tail-lift	1996
4567B	N236 EOR	Vauxhall Astra 1. 7LSD	Van	1995
4570F	N698 FWT	Ford Transit 190	Dropside lorry + double cab	1996
4571F	N889 PJV	Ford Transit 190	Dropside lorry + double cab	1996
4572F	N890 PJV	Ford Transit 190	Dropside lorry + crew-cab	1996
4573F	N403 PFU	Ford Transit 190	Van	1995
4574F	N404 PFU	Ford Transit 190	Van	1995
4575F	N405 PFU	Ford Transit 190	Van	1996
4576F	N518 PJV	Ford Transit	12-seat minibus	1996
4577F	N418 PFU	Ford Transit 100	Van	1995
4578F	N417 PFU	Ford Transit 100	Van	1995
4579F	N416 PFU	Ford Transit 100	Van	1995
4580F	N26 UKV	Ford Escort 1. 8D	5-door estate car	1995
4581F	N419 PFU	Ford Transit 190	Van	1996
4582B	N289 SPJ	Vauxhall Astra 1. 6LS	Van	1995
4583B	N287 SPJ	Vauxhall Astra 1. 6 Auto	Van	1995
4584B	N288 SPJ	Vauxhall Astra 1. 6LS	Van	1995
4585F	N420 PFU	Ford Transit 190 LWB	Van	1995
4587F	N731 FWT	Ford Transit 190	Dropside lorry + crew-cab/tail-lift	1996
4588F	N476 RBE	Ford Transit 190	Van	1996
4589F	N475 PJV	Ford Transit 190	Van	1996
4590F	P727 HHJ	Ford Escort 1. 6LX	5-door estate car	1996
4591F	N968 GMJ	Ford Escort 1. 6LX	5-door estate car	1996
4592B	P894 RUU	Vauxhall Astra	Van	1996
4594F	N516 CTM	Ford Escort 1. 8LD	5-door estate car	1996
4595F	N460 RBE	Ford Transit 100	Van	1996
4596F	N859 PJV	Ford Transit	12-seat minibus	1996
4597F	N472 RBE	Ford Transit 190	Dropside lorry + crew-cab/tail-lift	1996
4598F	N447 RBE	Ford Escort 1. 8D	Van	1996
4599F	N448 RBE	Ford Escort 35	Van	1996
4600F	N468 RBE	Ford Transit 190	Dropside lorry + crew-cab/tail-lift	1996
4601F	N547 ARW	Ford Escort 1. 6LX	5-door estate car	1996
4602F	N546 ARW	Ford Escort 1. 8LXD	5-door estate car	1996
4667F	N449 RBE	Ford Escort 1. 8D	Van	1996

4668B	N136 OYX	Vauxhall Vectra 2. 0GLS	Van	1996
4670F	N68 KVG	Ford Transit 190	Van	1996
4671F	N247 RBE	Ford Transit 190	Dropside lorry + crew-cab	1996
4672F	P504 NPW	Ford Transit 150	Semi-high-top van	1996
4673F	P505 NPW	Ford Transit 150	Semi-high-top van	1996
4674F	N789 NGJ	Ford Escort 1. 8D	Van	1996
4675F	N790 NGJ	Ford Escort 1. 8D	Van	1996
4676B	N183 OYX	Vauxhall Astra 1. 6iLS	Van	1996
4677F	N792 XAC	Ford Escort 1. 6iLX	5-door estate car	1996
4678F	P513 PGK	Ford Transit 190	Van	1996
4679F	P514 PGK	Ford Transit 190	Van	1996
4680F	N239 RBE	Ford Transit 100	Van	1996
4681F	N240 RBE	Ford Transit 100	Van	1996
4682F	N241 RBE	Ford Transit 100	Van	1996
4683F	P608 NPW	Ford Transit 190	Dropside lorry + crew-cab/tail-lift	1996
4684F	N128 HLW	Ford Transit 190	Dropside lorry + crew-cab/tail-lift	1996
4685F	N763 JVF	Ford Transit 190	Van	1996
4686F	N742 HLT	Ford Escort 55D	Van	1996
4687F	N289 KCL	Ford Transit 190	LTB mobile information office	1996
4688B	N885 GBK	Vauxhall Astra 1. 4 Merit	5-door estate car	1996
4690F	N123 HLW	Ford Transit 100	Van	1996
4691F	N121 HLW	Ford Transit 190	Van	1996
4692F	N658 JLD	Ford Transit 100	Van	1996
4693F	P737 LLX	Ford Transit 190	Van	1996
4694F	N137 HLW	Ford Transit 190	Van	1996
4695F	P736 LLX	Ford Transit 190	Van	1996
4696F	P735 LLX	Ford Transit 100	Van	1996
4697F	P734 LLX	Ford Transit 100	Van	1996
4698B	P194 JOW	Vauxhall Astra 1. 6 Merit Auto	5-door estate car	1996
4699F	N127 HLW	Ford Transit	12-seat minibus	1996
4700F	N661 JLD	Ford Transit 190	Dropside lorry + double cab/tail-lift	1996
4701F	N132 HLW	Ford Transit 100	Van	1996
4702F	N690 MTC	Ford Escort 1. 8D	Van	1996
4704B	N261 HPO	Vauxhall Astra 1. 6LS	5-door estate car	1996
4705F	P753 LLX	Ford Transit 190	Dropside lorry + tail-lift	1996
4706F	P752 LLX	Ford Transit 190	Dropside lorry + tail-lift	1996
4707F	P750 LLX	Ford Transit 190	Dropside lorry + tail-lift	1996
4709F	P751 LLX	Ford Transit 190	Dropside lorry + tail-lift	1996
4710F	N211 JLM	Ford Transit 100	Van	1996
4711F	N212 JLM	Ford Transit	15-seat minibus	1996
4713F	N213 JLM	Ford Transit 190	Van	1996
4714F	N214 JLM	Ford Transit 190	Van	1996
4715F	P749 LLX	Ford Transit 190	Van	1996
4717F	P532 PGJ	Ford Galaxy 2. 0GLXI	7-seat 'multi-purpose vehicle'	1996
4719F	P254 KKY	Ford Transit 190 LWB	Van	1996
4727F	P742 JRW	Ford Mondeo 1. 8LX	5-door estate car	1996
4731F	P582 MGS	Ford Transit 190	Van	1996
4732F	P583 MGS	Ford Transit 190	Van	1996
RCL 2221	CUV 221C	AEC Routemaster	Mobile exhibition and cinema bus	1965

TRAILERS

T29	-	York	Semi-trailer	1987
T32	-	Crane Fruehauf	Step-frame semi-trailer	1983
T33	-	Crane Fruehauf	Platform semi-trailer	1983
T34	-	Crane Fruehauf	Platform semi-trailer	1983
T35	-	Crane Fruehauf	Platform semi-trailer	1983
T36	-	Crane Fruehauf	Platform semi-trailer	1983
T37	-	Crane Fruehauf	Platform semi-trailer	1983
T38	-	Crane Fruehauf	Platform semi-trailer	1983
T39	-	Crane Fruehauf	Platform semi-trailer	1983
T42	-	Seb International	Cable drum carrier	1985
T43	-	Seb International	Cable drum carrier	1987
T44	-	Crane Fruehauf	Platform semi-trailer	1990
T46	-	Cobul	Box trailer	1990
T49	-	East Kent	Trailer	1991
T53	-	Carrymaster	Uniform issue unit trailer	1993
T54	-	Carrymaster	Uniform issue unit trailer	1993
T55	-	Cobul	'Tow-a-Van' box trailer	1993
T56	-	Cobul	Box trailer	1993
T57	-	Cobul	'Tow-a-Van' box trailer	1993
T58	-	Cobul	'Tow-a-Van' box trailer	1993
T59	-	Boden	Trailer	1994
T60	-	Extendable	Step-frame trailer	1995
T61	-	Challenger	Car transporter	1995
T62	-	Crane Fruehauf	Trailer	1995

Note: Trailers are numbered in a common series and officially prefixed 'T', but many actually carry prefixes relating to their manufacturer – e. g. T37 is numbered 'CT37'. Demountable bodies of varying types are also owned for use on certain lorry chassis, and have their own 'DB'-prefixed number series.

ABBREVIATIONS

Abbreviations used for Carbuilders

ABB	ABB Transportation (now ADtranz), Derby.
BREL	BREL Ltd, Derby (later became ABB Transportation Ltd).
Birmingham	Birmingham Railway Carriage & Wagon Company Ltd.
Bombardier	Bombardier Prorail Ltd., Horbury, Wakefield
Cravens	Cravens Ltd, Sheffield.
Derby	British Railways Workshops, Derby.
Gloucester	Gloucester Railway Carriage & Wagon Company Ltd.
Metro-Cammell	Metropolitan-Cammell Carriage & Wagon Company Ltd, Birmingham, now GEC-Alsthom Metro-Cammell Ltd.
Pickering	R. Y. Pickering & Company, Wishaw, Lanarkshire.
RFS	RFS Industries, Doncaster.

Other Abbreviations used:

ATO	Automatic Train Operation
ATP	Automatic Train Protection
BR	British Railways (later British Rail)
BRML	British Rail Maintenance Ltd
CDU	Cab Display Unit
CSDE	Correct Side Door Enable
CCTV	Closed Circuit Television
ETT	Experimental Tube Train
ERU	Emergency Response Unit
GEC	General Electric Company
JLE	Jubilee Line Extension
LNER	London & North Eastern Railway
LT	London Transport
LUL	London Underground Limited
NLR	North London Railways
NSE	Network SouthEast
OPO	One-Person Operation
PLS	Programme Logic System
TEP	Train Equipment Panel
TMS	Train Monitoring System